Short Historical Sketches of Page County, Virginia and Its People

Volume 2

A Collection of Articles from the
"Heritage and Heraldry" Column of the
Page News & Courier
October 2001–October 2004

Written and Compiled by
Robert H. Moore, II

HERITAGE BOOKS
2020

HERITAGE BOOKS

AN IMPRINT OF HERITAGE BOOKS, INC.

Books, CDs, and more—Worldwide

For our listing of thousands of titles see our website
at
www.HeritageBooks.com

Published 2020 by
HERITAGE BOOKS, INC.
Publishing Division
5810 Ruatan Street
Berwyn Heights, Md. 20740

Heritage Books by the author:

Short Historical Sketches of Page County, Virginia and Its People,
Volume 1: A Collection of Articles from the "Heritage and Heraldry" Column of the Page News & Courier,
August 1997–September 2001

Volume 2: A Collection of Articles from the "Heritage and Heraldry" Column of the Page News & Courier,
October 2001–October 2004

Cover illustration from a postcard c.1920
"Along the Shenandoah River, near Luray, Virginia"
published by Grove & McKay, Luray, Virginia

International Standard Book Numbers
Paperbound: 978-0-7884-3594-2
Clothbound: 978-0-7884-6404-1

Dedication

To My Grandparents

Harry G. and Myra F. Mayes Hilliard

A Note to the Reader

I am pleased to deliver this second installment of *Short Historical Sketches of Page County, Virginia and Its People*, with just over one hundred articles that I wrote for the *Page News & Courier* from October 2001 through October 2004. The articles are somewhat more diverse than those in the first volume, and deal with historic topics that reach into the twentieth century. However, biographical sketches and genealogical profiles continue to be an important aspect of this series. As additional volumes are compiled from the "Heritage & Heraldry" columns in the future, I hope to uncover new information about how the people of Page County lived over the past 270-plus years.

As ever I want to thank Jeb Caudill, Editor and General Manager of the *Page News & Courier,* for continuing to support the "Heritage & Heraldry" column and allowing the reprint of the articles in this series of books. Judy Campbell also merits significant thanks for conveniently compiling county records in a way that enables me to piece together genealogical data when writing a genealogical or biographical sketch. Thanks also are extended to all those who may contribute either in giving information or in giving an idea, sometimes in such subtle form that they don't even realize they have sparked an interest in me to conduct more research on a particular topic.

R.H.M., II
March 2, 2005

TABLE OF CONTENTS

Pre-Colonial, Early Colonial & the Revolution (16 articles)

Early & Antebellum Page County (16 articles)

Travel

Slavery

Early Life

American Civil War (29 articles)

World War I (10 articles)

Post WW1 Military (3 articles)

Surnames & Genealogical Research Tools (28 articles)

Miscellaneous (3 articles)

Pre-Colonial, Early Colonial & the Revolution

The Background of the Name 'Shenandoah'
(Pre-18th Century)
Article of 6/13/2002

The word "Shenandoah" has many potential roots, but one indisputable point is that it must have originated from Native American history. Senedo, Cenantua, Sherando, Gerando, and Shendo are just a few of the possibilities of the version "Shenandoah" that we are so familiar with these days. Some say that "Cenantua" referred to the Massanutten Mountain range; however it sounds a great deal like "Shenandoah."

Whatever the origin, the Senedo tribe is thought to have been the group of Native Americans that called our Valley home not long before the Europeans arrived. At some point in time however, Catawbas, from what became known as the Carolinas, attacked the Senedo along Smith Creek, in Shenandoah County. With the exception of one aged man and a young boy, the tribe was apparently wiped-out. According to one Benjamin Allen, a Quaker who settled in the area of Smith's Creek around 1734, an aged man of the Senedo often visited and told the Allens that the site of their farm was where the great massacre took place. If there is validity to the Allen family story of the aged man, while hunting and warring parties frequented the area well into the 1760s, it would seem that the Senedo were the last Native Americans to have resided on a regular basis in the Valley prior to the 1720s, maybe even earlier.

Still, even before the arrival of the Europeans, the hold that the Catawbas had on the Valley was apparently short-lived. Bands of the Delaware tribe crossed into the Valley by way of the gaps of the Blue Ridge Mountains and opened an intermittent war that lasted fore several years.

Apparently, even before the time of the Senedo and the ongoing fight between the Catawba and Delaware, the Cherokee were believed to have resided for a while in the Valley. A northern tribe too apparently drove them out, likely the Iroquois, even before the Europeans came.

Another interesting story about early Native American life in the Valley ties into Chief Powhatan of Jamestown fame. Opecancanough, a son of the Powhatan chief, was said to have made war on the Iroquois chief Sherando and drove them out. Opecancanough placed his son, Sheewanee, in charge of the area but was driven out by yet another attack and fled to the Tidewater.

Opecancanough returned to the to the Valley then and swept down on Sherando through a gap in the Blue Ridge, killing him and re-establishing his son.

Truly lost to time are the many stories of the Native Americans in the Valley, but many traces of their existence in the Valley are still evident today, from the arrowheads turned up in plowing fields, to what remains of many "Indian Mounds" in Page County.

Lastly, while many know "Shenandoah" as the "Daughter of the Stars." There is also reference to the name as "Daughter of the Moon."

Page County's Lineage as a Virginia County (1634-1831) Article of 6/24/2004

When tracing one's family tree, the researcher has to be ever mindful of the fact that Page County was not always called "Page County" and, while ancestors may have appeared to move from county to county until they finally came to roost in Page, they may have been here for quite a number of years, having settled in the area when it was known by another county name.

As many know, Page County was not actually formed until March 30, 1831, from portions of both Shenandoah and Rockingham Counties. Page was named for John Page, who had served as lieutenant governor of Virginia during the American Revolution and later as a member of the First U.S. Congress and as governor of Virginia. Shenandoah contributed 230 square miles while Rockingham contributed approximately 84 square miles from its northeast corner. Both Shenandoah and Rockingham County had been formed in 1778 in the midst of the American Revolution.

While Rockingham (named for the Marquis of Rockingham who had been a British statesman) had been formed from Augusta County (formed in 1738), Shenandoah had been formed from Dunmore County – a name that many found offensive due to the nature of the name being derived from the Lord Dunmore, who, was anything but sympathetic to the idea of American Independence. For Lord Dunmore's October 1777 decision to stand against the colonists, one of the delegates from the county stated that "his constituents no longer wished to live in, or he to represent, a county bearing the name of such a Tory; he theretofore moved to call it Shenandoah, after the beautiful stream that passes through it." Dunmore County had only existed since 1772, and, before that, it was better known as Frederick County.

Both Frederick County (formed in 1743 and named for Frederick Louis, Prince of Wales and eldest son of King George II) and Augusta County (formed in 1738) were formed from Orange County, which had been established in 1734. An unlikely derivation of the county name, one source states that the name came "from the color of the soil in its upper or mountainous portion."

However, it is more likely that the county actually derived its name from the Prince of Orange, who, in 1734, actually had married Princess Anne, daughter of King George II).

Orange County had originally been a part of Spotsylvania County. Established in 1720/1721, Spotsylvania County had been formed from Essex, King & Queen (formed from New Kent County in 1691) and King William (formed from King & Queen County in 1702) Counties and had been named for Alexander Spotswood, then governor of Virginia. Of course, Spotswood was also famous for his venture across the Blue Ridge and for his "Knights of the Golden Horseshoe" who had made that particular journey.

Essex County was formed in 1692 from Old Rappahannock County (not to be confused with the present Rappahannock County which was formed in 1833 from Culpeper County). In turn, Old Rappahannock County (which existed from 1656 – 1692) was formed from Lancaster County. Lancaster County had been formed in 1651 from both Northumberland and York Counties. Northumberland (formed between 1645 and 1648) was named for a county in England and was originally known as Chickcoun. Northumberland originally comprised the "whole neck of lands between Rappahannock and Potomac Rivers."

York County (1643) was originally named Charles River County and was one of the eight original shires formed in 1634.

What Lay Beneath
18th Century Native American Raids in the Area, Part 1 (1650 – 1756)
Article of 10/11/2001

Inevitably, the phrase "the victor writes the history," applies to Native Americans and their role in the history of the United States. Therefore, today, objectivity needs to be considered when writing about the history of the same to prevent a return to the passionate romanticist ideals that readily flowed in early 20th century works.

In addition to the much-enjoyed nostalgic flare of the romanticists, there is significant value to the various stories written by John Wayland, Harry Strickler and Joseph Waddell. There can be no doubt that what they transcribed (and much that remains unpublished in their notes), saved crucial Valley history that would have otherwise been lost. Additionally, to that list, it is also essential to include Samuel Kercheval.

Since the times of their published works, many resources have come to the surface to clarify various details. While the recorded raids were certainly tragic on the first American frontier, a different form of historiography has risen that enables us to, especially when it comes to Native Americans, become more objective and allows us to realize just what these people were trying to preserve in ridding their frontier of the "invasive Europeans."

It is possible that at the time of the settlement of Jamestown that there were actually Native Americans inhabiting the Shenandoah Valley. Sometime between 1650-1700, there may have been a group of people known as the "Senedo" (a possible origin of "Shenandoah?") that were exterminated by a Southern tribe – perhaps the Catawba.

Waddell even writes of Alexander Wither's beliefs of a group of people known as the Massawomees. In his 1831 work titled *Chronicles of Border Warfare*. Withers mentioned that when Virginia became known to the whites, the portion of the State lying northwest of the Blue Ridge and extending to the lakes was possessed by these people. "These were a powerful confederacy, rarely in unity with the tribes east of that range of mountains; but generally harassing them by frequent hostile irruptions into their country." As Europeans moved in-land from the coast, the Massawomee receded like the tide beyond the mountains.

As evidence of early Native Americans, though more likely the remains of yet an even earlier group of people, there were over 24 Native American burial mounds in Page County. Regretfully, the mounds were plowed through, robbed and excavated well into the 20th century and, much like the history of Native Americans in the Valley, the bulk of the rich artifacts from these mounds is not likely be found within the limits of the county's boundaries today.

Ultimately, as Europeans settled in the rich fertile areas of the Shenandoah Valley, and under the shadow of the Massanutten, there was the inevitability of a collision of cultures. For years before the first settlements, the Valley had been used as a hunting and trading arena as well as a route for warring tribes.

As early as 1742, there had been a clash between settlers and Native Americans in what is now Rockbridge County.

With the defeat of General Edward Braddock near Fort Duquesne in the summer of 1755, the gateway to the Valley seemed to be open for raids. In the spring of 1756, Native Americans appeared, according to Kercheval, in the lower Shenandoah Valley along the Potomac. Soon after, Fort Loudoun was constructed near Winchester.

What Lay Beneath
18th Century Native American Raids in the Area
Part 2
(1757 – 1765)
Article of 10/25/2001

As the way to the Valley seemed to have opened to Native American raids after 1755, the first of the hardest to impact the central Shenandoah Valley did not occur until 1758 – seemingly a pivotal year for raids. At least two chiefs – "Killbuck" and "the Crane" were credited with several of the raids during that time.

Both Rockingham and Shenandoah County bore witness to several raids. Yet, the area that would become known as Page County sustained a single raid, resulting in the Stone family "massacre." Wayland asserted that because of Page County's location, it was not attacked as much as other areas in the Valley, likely due to the county being "less exposed to incursions from the west and northwest."

By 1759, Native American raids seemed to come to an end, perhaps due to the French abandoning Fort Duquesne and Quebec being captured.

While scattered activity continued to take place in the Southern Valley, after the conclusion of the French and Indian War, the next series of raids to strike the central Valley did not occur until 1764. These raids were likely a "spin-off" result of the "uprising" of Chief Pontiac.

In what appears to have been a joined series of events, the John Dellinger family and George Miller families were struck first near Strasburg, followed by the Rhoades family in present Page County. Apparently, these raids may have been attributed, in part, to a "white scoundrel" amidst a group of Native Americans.

One source states the "scoundrel" to have been the notorious Simon Girty. However, by the time of the 1764 raids, and according to various biographies, it seems unlikely. Additionally, his "despised" and notorious practices" did not begin until the American Revolution.

After the summer of raids, the attacks seemed to roll back to the areas around Buffalo Gap, Churchville, Woodstock and Narrow Passage. Pontiac, lacking the support of the French, called for a peace that seemed to seal history of Native American raids in, at least, what would become Page County.

In 1768, Lewis Bingaman, a nephew of the Bingaman family attacked in 1758 in New Market, returned to the Massanutten area. Having been captured in 1758, Bingaman had become a "man of distinction" among the Native Americans.

Making himself known to Frederick Offenbacker, Bingaman stated that he was looking for John Price. According to an account related to John Wayland, Price was a "skilled hunter and marksman" who had made friends with an Indian chief, but had killed him and carried off his rifle and other possessions. Upon returning to the Hawksbill, Price apparently boasted of the episode. Bingaman told Offenbacker, "I have thirty warriors hidden up yonder in Massanutten Gap. If we can get Price, nobody else will be harmed. If we don't get him we'll kill the first white people we can find." Offenbacker agreed to cooperate. Subsequently, Price was decoyed into the mountain and never heard from again.

While a definitive tie has yet to have been proved, Lewis may have been the father of George Bingaman (born ca. 1770), who in turn, fathered Mary (born ca. 1815) who married John J. Koontz, a grandson of Elder John Koontz, in Page County in 1829.

By 1774, amidst the conflict known as Dunmore's War, the fight for America's first frontier had taken a turn when the colonists began to take the fight in earnest to the Native Americans.

The Struggle to Leave Europe – Early Lives of the Rothgeb/Roadcap and Good Families, Part 1 (1730s) Article of 2/7/2002

The progenitor of Page County Rothgebs, Hans Jacob Radtgab, is believed to have been born July 29, 1708, the son of Jacob and Elizabeth Rinderknecht Rathgeb.

It is unclear whether or not Casper Gut (Good) – also of Zurich, like Radtgab – was a good acquaintance of Radtgab's, but by age 19, Casper was in the company of Hans Jacob as the Rev. Maurice Goetschy ministry prepared to leave Zurich, Switzerland for America.

According to the Zurich newspaper, *Nachrihten von Zurich*, the group left on Oct. 4, 1734. In addition to accounting for Radtgab's journey, it gives an excellent impression of what many German and Swiss immigrants must have experienced.

Consisting of a "considerable number of country people, old and young," the group appears to have been, at first, bound for "Carolina island." It seems that they may have been referring to the already existing colony (1710) of Swiss at what is now known as New Bern, North Carolina. Despite being "urgently dissuaded" by government officials and local clergy, Goetschy "persisted in his resolution, and took his departure. "Following his departure, yet another boat of what the newspaper referred to as 174 "silly people" took their leave of Switzerland.

"Many thousands saw them depart with great pity for them, especially because they were under-taking so thoughtlessly, with wife and child, and but poorly provided for, the dangerous journey of 300 hours in cold, rain and wind, now, when the days are getting shorter. Nevertheless, kindhearted and distinguished persons supplied them with all kinds of articles, such as bread, shawls, caps, etc. The following day the third boat started off. These were liberally provided from the office of charities, with a large amount of bread, flour, stockings and other supplies. Especially the neighborhood of the exchange showed itself deeply sympathetic;

nor will they be likely to forget what was given to them at the Salthouse for bodily refreshment. In like manner many merchants assisted them. Upon the last boat were 82 persons, who would have been worthy of more consideration if they had been compelled to leave for the honor or the truth of God. They must bear the consequences of their act, be they good or ill."

Ultimately, "upwards of 20" were "induced by the wise representations of worthy gentlemen and citizens" to change "their intentions" and remained behind and were "very kindly returned to their homes." The paper concluded in saying, "Meanwhile we should pray God that the great number who have gone on this journey, may either soon return or reach the destination they so much wish for. May He fill their hearts with patience, and, as many sad hours are likely to embitter their voyage, may He comfort them with the thought that, if they remain faithful, a far better life is reserved for them"

The journey down the Rhine is told of "at length in a pamphlet which Ludwig Webber, one of the emigrants who returned to Zurich from Holland, wrote and published at Zurich in 1735 as a warning to later venturesome spirits."

Webber wrote:

"The emigrants turned from Zurich northward till they reached the Rhine at Laufenburg. Then taking a boat on the Rhine they came, on October 5, to Rheinfelden, where they had to show their passports. Towards evening of the same day they reached Basle (Basel). There they had to wait until a passport could be secured from Comte du Jour, the commanding general of the French army at Strassburg."

The Struggle to Leave Europe – Early Lives of the Rothgeb/Roadcap and Good Families, Part 2 (1730s) Article of 2/21/2002

With a need to secure a passport at Basle, the Goetschy emigrants were blessed by the kindness of a gentleman of that village who paid the 44 guilders so that the emigrants could secure one and continue their trek. However, it took two more days before their ship arrived to carry them down the Rhine.

As they awaited the arrival of the ship, many became impatient and took the advice of a tailor from Lichensteg, taking the road through France. "Thirty-one persons followed him, but nothing more was heard of them. Another "forty to fifty others resolved to travel through Lorraine by way of Namur to Rotterdam." Seeking alms along the way, and despite many "quarrels and difficulties," this group actually arrived at Rotterdam eight days after the main party that waited for the ship.

Webber's account of the shipboard journey from Basle continued: "At Basle eighty refuges from Piedmont joined them in a separate ship. The main party, consisting of 194 persons, embarked in two ships. They suffered intensely on the ships through rain and cold, against which they were but poorly protected with scanty clothes and provisions."

"After leaving Basle their first encampment was upon an island, covered with trees and shrubs, in the middle of the Rhine. Such continued to be their night quarters, although the nights were wet and cold. Moreover the ships were crowded so badly that there was hardly enough room to sit, much less to lie down. There was no opportunity for cooking on the ships; and as they were sometimes compelled to stay days and nights on the ships, the cries of the children were pitiful and heartrending. Whenever they could get ashore they cooked, warmed themselves and dried their clothes. Many would have liked to return home, but as the armies of the French and the Austrians lay on both sides of the river, they did not dare risk it. Quarrels among men and women were frequent. Mrs. Goetschy, the chronicler tells us, often quarreled with her husband, called him all kinds of names and one morning tore a cane from his hand and belabored his back soundly."

"At night they saw the camp fires of the imperial troops on one side and of the French on the other, which terrified them by their ghostly appearance. As they were afraid of an attack from one or both armies almost at any time, they refrained carefully from making the least noise, so as to pass by unnoticed. Nevertheless, they were stopped repeatedly. At Old Breysach, in the Breisgau, all their chests were opened and examined. Goetschy, who called on the commandant of the fort, was advised to leave immediately, as the French on the other side of the river were aiming three field pieces at the boats. Of course they made off with all possible speed. At Ketsch, near Schwetzingen, west of Heidelberg, the dragoons of the imperial army stopped the boats and compelled Mr. Wirtz of Zurich, who acted as self-appointed commissary, to go to Heidelberg and secure a passport for 30 guilders, from the Duke of Wurtemberg, the commanding general of the imperial army. They were also forced to make an extra payment of two ducats for each vessel.

The Struggle to Leave Europe – Early Lives of the Rothgeb/Roadcap and Good Families, Part 3 (1730s)

Article of 3/7/2002

At the mercy of the imperial army, the Goetschy emigrants, including Conrad Gut and Hans Jacob Radtgab, still had many trials ahead of them.

"Nine miles below the Mayence the dragoons again rode after them and would not have allowed them to pass on, if their leader had not been of the Reformed religion. They took the meat away from Goetschy's plate with their sabers, which they swung about his head, so that he quite lost his appetite. Shortly before reaching Mayence from forty to fifty men had exhausted all their money, so that they did not even have enough to pay their boat fare. They were compelled to continue the journey on foot."

"At Mayence they were delayed four days because they could not agree with the captain of the boats about the passage money to be paid to Rotterdam. Finally they agreed on three guilders for adults and half fare for children."

"After leaving Mayence their journey was a little more comfortable, for they had at least a chance to cook on the ships. Their spiritual needs, however, were sadly neglected, for, if we can believe the chronicler of the journey, the pastor, Mr. Goetschy, always had the pipe or the wineglass near his mouth. Mornings and evenings, one of the men, Heinrich Scheuchzer from Zurich, read a prayer. When Goetschy actually did preach a sermon, in which he compared some of the leaders of the company to the followers of Korah, Dathan and Abiram, he almost caused a riot."

When the group reached Neuweid, Westerwald, Bavaria four couples of the Goetschy ministry were married by a Reformed minister. Among those were Hans Jacob Radtgab and Barbara Haller, "both of Walliselen." The daughter of Hans George and Ana Gafallenberg Haller, Barbara married Hans Jacob on October 28, 1734.

Once this happy event had concluded, the journey prepared to continue. However, "The Count of Wied desired them to remain in his territory, offering to give them houses and land, but as he did not promise as much as they expected to receive in Carolina, they did not accept his offer, but left."

"From Neuwied they continued their journey down the Rhine until they reached Collenburg (now Culenborg) in Holland. There they were compelled to stop four days because of a strong contrary wind. Goetschy was invited to preach in the principal church in Culenborg, which he did with much acceptance. As a result a collection was taken up by the congregation for the party, so that each received one guilder. From Culenborg Goetschy sent, a party of three men to Rotterdam, where he said two English ships were waiting for them. At Culenborg they also sold their ships, which they must have bought at Basle, for 45 Dutch guilders, apparently a very small sum. Then, contrary to their agreement, they were compelled to take another ship to convey them to Rotterdam. In their hurry to get off several children fell overboard into the water, from which they were rescued with difficulty. Early the following morning they reached Rotterdam."

"Having reached Rotterdam they heard to their dismay that no ships were waiting for them. Moreover the captain of the ship with which they had come wished to return at once, so they had to unload their goods quickly and, having no other place, they dumped them on the bank of the river in one heap."

The Struggle to Leave Europe –
Early Lives of the Rothgeb/Roadcap and Good Families,
Part 4
(1730s)
Article of 3/21/2002

While awaiting a ship at Rotterdam, the fate of the Goetschy emigrants seemed filled with uncertainty. A glimmer of hope seemed to shine through when Goetschy received a letter from someone at the Hague, asking Goetschy to come to the Hague.

A few days after Goetschy's departure, one of the group who had accompanied the leader returned with great "news that several oxen would be sent to them from the Hague, that the States General would send them to England at their own expense and that a large sum of money had been collected for them in England."

Again, the group was subject to false hope as none of the news came to fruition. To make matters worse, a few days later Goetschy returned to announce that the State's General had offered him "a position as a minister of great importance, that he and his family had thus received unexpected help and he advised them to secure similar help for themselves."

Almost at once, many resorted to begging for help. However, with the magistrate's threat of a fine of 25 guilders, this practice stopped immediately. With no resources and moving into a harsh period of cold weather, many "became sick from want and hunger, and two of them died."

Webber continued to describe the ordeal:

"A tailor from Buchs, Sebastian Neracher by name, who was married in Rotterdam, came to see them. Most of them were in an inn outside of the city. He took care of those from Buchs. He brought with him a Mr. Schapenhaudt, who interceded for them so successfully that many people took pity on them and distributed food and clothes among them. They also paid for their lodgings at the inn."

"Mr. Schapenhaudt presented their sad condition to Rev. Wilhelmi of Rotterdam, who advised them to go to the Hague and apply there to Mr. Von Felss, at the English embassy, to present their needy condition to him. Three men were sent to the Hague. When they reached the Hague, they first hunted up Mr. Goetschy and told him of their intention. He was greatly displeased with their plan and told them he had already spoken with Mr. Felss, who was sufficiently well informed about their plans and condition. Goetschy entertained the three men at dinner and then offered to send a letter with them to Mr. Wilhelmi at Rotterdam. After waiting an hour for the letter, he sent them word that he had already dispatched it with his boy. Hence they had to return to Rotterdam without having accomplished their purpose."

"When Goetschy had received from Mr. Felss the assurance of his appointment as minister to Pennsylvania, he returned to Rotterdam and acquainted his party of emigrants with his changed plans. Most of them readily accepted his proposal to change their destination from Carolina to Pennsylvania. There were, however, some who refused to have anything to do with him."

Finally, on February 24, 1735, 88 members of the party boarded a ship for England, never to be heard from again. The remaining 143 persons signed their names for passage to Philadelphia and agreed with the owner of a ship (Schiffpatron) to pay six doubloons per adult and three per child. Additionally, a pledge was made between all in the party to pay the passage money of any who might die in transit.

What lay ahead in the voyage to England and America follows.

The Struggle to Leave Europe – Early Lives of the Rothgeb/Roadcap and Good Families, Part 5 (1730s)

Article of 4/4/2002

Finally bound for the British Isles, the party that included Casper Gut and the Radtgabs, must have felt some sort of exhilaration to finally depart mainland Europe. Regretfully, that feeling was probably short-lived. The journey itself was detailed in a latter written by Goetschy's son, John Henry Goetschy, then a boy of 17 years:

"After we had left Holland and surrendered ourselves to the wild, tempestuous ocean, its waves and its changeable winds, we reached, through God's great goodness toward us, with good wind, England within 24 hours. After a lapse of two days we came to the island of Wicht [Wight] and there to a little town, called Caus [Cowes], where our captain supplied himself with provisions for the great ocean [trip] and we secured medicines for this wild sea."

Aboard the *Mercury*, the company of 186 passengers in-all, including 61 men, 51 women, 37 boys and 34 girls sailed from Cowes "under God's goodness, with a good east wind away from there."

Goetschy's son described the trip – "When we had left the harbour and saw this dreaded ocean, we had a favorable wind only for the following day and the following night. Then we had to hear a terrible storm and the awful roaring and raging of the waves when we came into the Spanish and Portuguese ocean. For twelve weeks we were subjected to this misery and had to suffer all kinds of bad and dangerous storms and terrors of death, which seemed to be even more bitter than death. With these we were subject to all kinds of bad diseases. The food was bad, for we had to eat what they call 'galley bread.' We had to drink stinking, muddy water, full of worms. We had an evil tyrant and rascal for our captain [William Wilson was the master] and first mate, who regarded the sick as nothing else than dogs. If one said: 'I have to cook something for a sick man,' he replied: 'Get away from here or I'll throw you overboard, what do I care for your sick devil.' In short, misfortune is everywhere upon the sea. We alone fared better. This has been the experience of all who have come to this land and even if a king traveled across the sea, it would not change. After having been in this misery sufficiently long, God, the Lord, brought us out and showed us the land, which caused great joy among us. But three days passed, the wind being contrary, before we could enter into the right river. Finally a good south wind came and brought us one day through the glorious Telewa [Delaware], which is a little larger than the Rhine, but not by far as wild as the latter, because this country has no mountains, to the long expected and wished for city of Philadelphia."

Finally, almost eight months after leaving Switzerland, Philadelphia was reached on May 29, 1735.

Goetschy's people had made it.

After the Trip, the Early Rothgeb and Good Families of Page County
Article of 4/18/2002
(1731 – 1752)

Following the trip across the Atlantic, Jacob Rothgeb's passage was paid by Joseph Strickler, who, in turn, Jacob was indentured for seven years. Then, according to *Papa's Diary* by Rita Rothgeb White (published in Luray in 1961), Jacob may have been indentured an additional seven years for the passage of his wife.

The "Joseph Strickler of Egypt" tie should not be confused with the one born in 1731, but refers to a younger brother of Abraham "the Pioneer." The Joseph Strickler that is referred to in relation with Hans Jacob Rothgeb's indenture was born ca. 1680 while Abraham "the Pioneer" was born ca. 1670.

In September 1749, after his years of servitude, Jacob received a grant from Lord Fairfax for 400 acres in what was to become the Page Valley. According to Mrs. White, "The present road from Luray to the village of Leaksville is in the center of this grant."

Jacob and Barbara had several children including Hannah, Elizabeth, Barbara, Catherine and Peter. Following Barbara's death ca. 1740, Jacob married again in 1740 to Anna Neff or Gut. They had at least one child, John George Rothgeb, who appears to be the man responsible for a line of children that carried on the Rothgeb name to generations residing in the Page Valley today. Children of John George Rothgeb included Isaac, Abraham, Elizabeth, Jacob, David, Christian, George, Barbara, Samuel, Joseph, John, Anna, Michael, Esther, Reuben and Mary! Six of these children married Stricklers.

Speaking of the second marriage of Jacob, familiarity seemed to be an aspect among many early settlers of the Valley as "travelers" and their children married frequently amongst themselves. Specifically, one of the interesting marriages that occurred ca. 1758 was between one of Jacob's fellow Atlantic travelers, Casper Good, and his daughter, Catherine Rotecap (Rothgeb).

Interestingly, one child of Casper and Catherine was Jonas Good, who married Sarah Tanner. The Tanner family had anglicized their family name some years before from Gerber. Sarah's grandfather, Christopher had married Elizabeth Aylor, daughter of Anna Magdalena Aylor and the granddaughter of Henry Snyder and Dorothy, both 1717 Germanna colonists (continuing the ever-present ties of the Page Valley German settlers with the legacy of Spotswood's amazing Virginia German venture).

Hans Jacob Rothgeb died either in 1751 or 1752. As mentioned, he left quite a legacy to descendants that still carry the surname in the Page Valley. However, like so many other families in this area, he too had descendants, grandchildren, that left the Valley for lands in Ohio and beyond. One of John George Rothgeb's sons, Michael, settled and died in Mahoning County, Ohio.

Residents of the Germanna Colonies and Page County, Part 1 (1714 – 1716) Article of 9/16/2004

I have written several times about certain people from the Germanna Colony but have yet to explain the full impact that the colony had on aiding in populating the central Shenandoah Valley – most specifically, the area now known as Page County. While many focus credit on the German route of immigration from Pennsylvania to the Valley of Virginia, many seem to forget the role of Virginia Germans and their migratory pattern from just across the Blue Ridge at the Germanna Colonies.

As early as 1714, the first of three German colonies during the administration of Governor Alexander Spotswood settled not far east of the Blue Ridge in Orange County. Twelve families numbering 42 persons were among the first colony, designated by the Virginia Council in April 1714. All of these colonists belonged to the German Reformed Church and were natives of the old principality of Nassau-Siegen, now part of Westphalia, Germany. At Germanna, these settlers also organized the first congregation of the German Reformed Church in what became the United States. Among these early settlers were a few names now familiar in Page's history including the families of Koontz, Brumback, and Hoffman (and possibly Weaver and Martin).

According to the Kemper family genealogy, the 1714 settlers of Germanna "did not leave their homes not knowing where they were going, nor because they were compelled to. They were engaged to go, and knew where they were going, and what they were to do. They came from one of the thriftiest and most intelligent provinces of Germany; they were master mechanics, and were an intelligent, progressive, set of people."

Rev. Hugh Jones, in his *Present State of Virginia*, published about 1724, noted of Germanna, "above the Falls of the Rappahannock River, within view of the vast mountains, he has founded a town, called Germanna from the Germans sent over by Queen Anne . . . He has servants and workmen at most handicraft trades . . ." According to one 20th century history of the 1714 settlers, "they were fairly well educated people by the standards of the time. Compulsory schooling was introduced in Nassau-Siegen in the middle of the 16th century. All of this colony, excepting Haeger and Holtzclaw, were raised on farms and undoubtedly farmed land owned by them when they emigrated. Farm work was done by the women and children and at special seasons by the men who were taught mining and iron-working."

During his November 1715 visit of Germanna, John Fontaine gave an excellent account of what could be found in the early village;

"we walked about the town, which is palisaded with stakes stuck in the ground, and laid close the one to the other, and of substance to bear our a musket-shot. There are but nine families, and they have nine houses, built all in a line; and before every house, about twenty feet distant from it, they have small sheds built for their hogs and hens, so that the hog-sties and houses make a street. The place that is paled in is a pentagon, very regularly laid out; and in the very center there is a block-house, made with five sides, which answer to the five sides of the great inclosure; there are loop-holes through it, from which you may see all the sides of the inclosure. This was intended for a retreat for the people, in case they were not able to defend the palisades, if attacked by Indians."

Fontaine continued, "They make use of this block-house for divine service. They go to prayers constantly once a day, and have two sermons on Sunday. We went to hear them perform their service, which was done in their own language, which we did not understand; but they seemed to be very devout, and sang the psalms well."

By the time of Fontaine's second visit, in November 1716, Spotswood had not only had his famous adventure with the Knights of the Golden Horseshoe (August 1716) but had initiated his venture into mining silver – a venture that would prove fruitless.

Residents of the Germanna Colonies and Page County, Part 2 (1714 – 1774) Article of 9/23/2004

Focusing last week on the fact that at least six Page County families have genealogical links to the 1714 colony of Germanna (Koontz, Brumback, and Hoffman; and possibly Weaver and Martin; and I forgot to mention the Hitt family), this week we move along to 1717 when Germanna received yet a new set of colonists. As before with the 1714 colony, this later colony also had a number of families in it that would later have descendants settle in the area that would later become known as Page County, including the families of Broyles, Zimmerman, Snyder, Yaeger, Turner, and others.

Unlike the first set of colonists, when these Germans (twenty families of eighty persons) arrived they arrived as a matter of circumstance, originally intending Pennsylvania to be their ultimate destination. When the captain of the boat landed in Virginia, Spotswood paid for the passage of these Germans with the intent of reinforcing his colony in Orange County. These settlers hailed from a different part of Germany than those of the 1714 colony, coming from the Alsace, the Palatinate and adjacent districts in Germany. They also differed from the 1714 colonists in that the 1717 colonists were made up chiefly of Lutherans.

Two years later, yet a third colony (of forty families) would arrive in Germanna. Regretfully little is known about these families but there is certainly cause to believe that this group also had ties to later Page County families. As with the 1717 colonists, this group was composed mostly of Lutherans.

Shortly after the third colony the settlers, there is speculation that the 1714 colonists grew frustrated with Spotswood over things that he had done or promised to do and had not been done, and left Germanna in 1721, settling just a few miles south of Warrenton, on Licking Run in Fauquier County. Acquiring approximately 1,805 acres there, the village that was created from these relocated settlers was soon known as Germantown. One Moravian missionary who passed through the village in 1748 noted that it was "like a village in Germany where the houses are far apart." As early as 1731, members of the Germantown settlement obtained a grant for 50,000 acres of land in the Shenandoah Valley. One publication on the history of the Germanna Colony states that this land rested "between the Blue Ridge and the Shenandoah River, in the present counties of Warren and Page."

Following in the 1714 colonists footsteps somewhat, around 1725 or 1726, the 1717 and 1719 Germanna colonists also relocated, but to Madison County – having fulfilled their indenture to Gov. Spotswood. Taking up land on the Robinson River and the White Oak Run, these former Germanna colonists soon established a log church, known as the German Chapel – the forerunner of the famous Hebron Church. The first minister of this church was Rev. Johannes Casper Stoever (ministered from 1733 – 1739), who most of the Koontz descendants can claim direct family ties. Following in Rev. Stoever's wake (following his death on the Atlantic after a successful effort in Germany to solicit funds and religious tracts) was Rev. George S. Klug (ministered from 1739 – 1764). Klug is believed to have made regular visits to the early settlers of Massanutten (the Flat Woods Church). Following Klug was the Rev. Johannes Schwarbach (ministered at Hebron from 1764 – 1774) who was known to have rendered pastoral services at Mt. Calvary (also known as the Hoxbiehl, or Gomers/Comer's Church) in the 1760s. On August 6, 1765, Schwarbach conveyed three acres of land to Peter Painter and Jacob Shaffer, trustees of Mt. Calvary.

Yet another church that appears to have been "intimately associated" with the Hebron Church was the Bethlehem Church (Pass Run Church), though records prior to 1851 cannot be found.

Inevitably, the land that now encompasses Page County was seen as a desirable relocation spot by many of the former Germanna colonists and their earliest descendants. Not only do the tracings of surnames testify to this but also the tracings of the earliest history of the Lutheran Church in Virginia. In one history of the church published in 1930, it was cited that Page County, next to Madison, has the earliest Lutheran history in Virginia. As of the 1916 census, Lutherans were shown "to be the second largest of church people in Page."

There is much more to the Germanna colonists that might be of interest to several readers and they are encouraged to surf the web for the Memorial Foundation for the Germanna Colonies in Virginia, Inc. Additionally, the snail-mail address for the foundation is "PO Box 279, Locust Grove, Va. 22508-0279. The foundation sells numerous publications that would be of interest to Germanna descendants.

An Early History of the Lutheran Churches in Page County (1720s – 1870s)
Article of 9/30/2004

As indicated in the history of the Germanna colony, the future Page County had many ties with early German Virginia settlers as well as those from Pennsylvania and Maryland. Naturally, one of the earliest Christian faiths in the area was, therefore, Lutheran. Both Flatwood's and Naked Creek Church were supposedly established within a decade after the establishment of the Massanutten settlement and Rev. George S. Klug, of the Hebron Church in Madison was visiting as early as 1748. Klug was extremely active in the Shenandoah Valley extending his ministry from Frederick County south to Rockingham. Known to have formed the Mt. Calvary Church, he may also be seen easily as the father of the Lutheran ministries throughout the Page Valley, as Mt. Calvary (also known as Hoxbiehl or Gomer's/Comer's Church, later proved to the be the mother church to many Page County after the 1860s. Not surprisingly, Rev. John Schwarbach followed Klug in prominence among the Page Valley Lutheran Churches, as he was also a successor to Klug at Hebron.

Rev. Schwarbach was originally a teacher near York, Pa. and desired to be licensed as a catechist "that he might extend his usefulness to some outlying districts under the supervision of the pastor residing in York." Granted permission by the Ministerium of Pennsylvania, Schwarbach successfully fulfilled the requirements and, following Klug's death in 1764, heard of the vacancy at Hebron. Traveling "to the distant point to learn for himself what the needs" of the congregation were, Schwarbach appeared before the Ministerium in 1766 with three letters from the congregation in Virginia, "commending him for his services among them and earnestly requesting that he be licensed so that he might perform all the ministerial acts in this distant field, separated by hundreds of miles from the homes of other Lutheran ministers." Granted a license to practice, Schwarbach arrived in Virginia in 1766 and preached at Hebron through 1774. According to the *History of the Lutheran Church*, Schwarbach "prosecuted the work as it had been carried out by his predecessor, which included the three congregations uniting in the request for his services. The work in the home congregation continued to prosper. Across the mountains he served Mt. Calvary, St. Peter's, and Peaked Mountain, designated in the letter as the church on Fort Run." Schwarbach continued with the Hebron Church and his works in the Valley until the spring of 1774. Little is known about his life for the four years between then and the next appearance in the Valley in 1768 when he was shown as preaching at the Peaked Mountain Church.

While the direct ties between Page's Lutheran congregations and Hebron seem to dissipate somewhat with Schwarbach's leaving the Hebron Church, the Lutheran Churches of the Page Valley would still be impacted in years to come by Schwarbach's preaching. In part, that extension over time came from Schwarbach's extending his ministry well into the western reaches of the Virginia frontier in the 1760s and 1770s. During that time he came in touch with the families of Jacob and his father Justus Henckel. The Henckel family, like many of the Germanna settlers, had roots in the Kraichgau area east of Heidelberg. In 1717, Rev. Anton Jacob Henckel, father of Justus, arrived in America and likely was responsible for organizing the first Lutheran congregations in Pennsylvania. Therefore, it seemed only natural that "Jacob and his father Justus," according to the *History of the Lutheran Church in Virginia*, "loved their Bible and their books of sermons." When Rev. Schwarbach arrived at the home, "conversations would turn gradually to spiritual things . . . and the children would sit by and listen." One of Jacob's children was Paul Henkel. "Paul Henkel tells us how he listened to the visiting pastor as he carried on a conversation with his father, Jacob, and he learned to listen to the public sermons, attended catechetical instruction and in 1768 Paul Henkel was confirmed by Pastor Schwarbach."

An Early History of the Lutheran Churches in Page County, Part 2 (1773 – 1873) Article of 10/7/2004

Completing his work in the catechism in 1768, sometime around 1784 Paul Henkel was preaching at the Hoxbiehl/Comer's Church, returning the legacy of the Hebron Church to the Page Valley. In the decade between Rev. Schwarbach's departure in 1774 and Rev. Henkel's arrival ca. 1784, there are some gaps in the history of the Lutheran ministry in Page County. It is known that Rev. John Peter Gabriel Muhlenberg administered to the Comer's Church congregation (1773) near the end of Schwarbach's ministry. However, there is somewhat of a mystery as to who was present for nearly ten years before John Michael Schmidt arrived. Known by Muhlenberg as the "Volunteer Preacher," Schmidt arrived at Hebron ca. 1782 at the approval of Rev. Muhlenberg. However, Paul Henkel pointed out that when he encountered Schmidt on the Hawksbill that he "had proved himself unworthy of the office to which he had been called, and how the Hebron elders had been forced to dismiss him." Henkel subsequently replaced Schmidt and served well into the 1790s before Rev. W.G. Forster arrived.

So far, this brief history of the Lutheran Church in the Page Valley has spanned the 1700s. However, what is most interesting at this point is seeing the Lutheran church's existence in the future Page County in an almost nucleus-like form with clearly traceable transitions of ministers from the time of the Germanna settlement, through Hebron to the establishment of Hoxbiehl-Gomer's/Comer's Church. Though intermittently interrupted by other ministers of the Lutheran faith from the Ministerium of Pennsylvania, in somewhat genealogical ascension, the Lutheran ministry in the Page Valley went from Rev. John Casper Stoever, Sr., to his son, Rev. John Casper Stoever, Jr. to Rev. Stoever Sr.'s replacement, the Rev. George Klug to Rev. Schwarbach and to the man he inspired - Rev. Paul Henkel, it is fascinating to see the evolution of the religion in the new world and the genesis of it truly taking place in the central Shenandoah Valley. But, it would not end with Rev. Paul Henkel.

Just as Schwarbach had influenced Paul Henkel, Rev. Henkel later saw a candidate for the ministry in one John George Schmucker, a son of a German immigrant family in Woodstock, Shenandoah County. According to the 1930 history of the Lutheran Church in Virginia, Schmucker "For a year . . . sat at the feet of his pastor Paul Henkel and studied the branches of learning that would help him to become a minister." After completing his studies in Philadelphia, Schmucker was licensed in 1792 and ordained in 1800. John George was but one of three siblings to enter into the ministry, and, the youngest brother, John Peter Schmucker, served as a minister at Mt. Calvary from 1817-1820. Another minister to come along, also under the influence of the "Germanna descendancy" was Rev. Jacob Stirewalt and yet other Henkel minister heirs such as Ambrose and Socrates Henkel.

Though I have followed the ministers in transition into the early 1800s, certainly two other churches cannot be forgotten in this brief overview of the Lutheran Church in the Page Valley. Almost certainly, Monger's Church (later known as St. Paul's) and the Stoneberger Church (formerly the Flatwoods Church and later St. Luke's) both shared the Lutheran ministry of both Hebron and Mt. Calvary through the late 1700s.

Though not considered a spin-off of Mt. Calvary, Monger's Church was a log church located on the west bank of the Shenandoah River, approximately one mile northeast of the present brick structure of St. Paul's and was formed ca. 1782. Apparently, in the time of Peter Schmucker's service to Mt. Calvary, he was also in the service of this church from 1818 – 1821.

As mentioned earlier, Stoneberger's Church (ca. 1795) was the likely continuation of Flatwoods church that once stood near Massanutten. Possibly known as William's Church or even St. William's Church prior to 1795, Stoneberger's Church was located on Stony Run where the Honeyville Road crosses the stream about two miles west of Stanley. As it was not uncommon to see local Lutheran churches serving both Lutherans and Reformist, Stoneberger's Church, like Monger's Church, was one. In 1873, the Lutheran's broke off from Stoneberger's and bought land at Alma where the present St. Luke's Lutheran Church now stands.

Captain Michael Rader's Company of Virginia Militia
(1775 – 1777)
Article of 12/13/2001

Many Page County descendants have genealogical ties to members of Rader's company and are aware of the little data that survived to document the service of the company. While there is no definite date of enlistment for the company, it was likely among the large number of units recruited in the summer of 1775. In the wake of Lexington and Concord, Congress had begun the enlistment of troops in New England, but had also encouraged the middle and southern states to do the same for their own defense.

By the summer of 1775, Virginia had been thrown into a frenzy, as the royal governor of Virginia, John Murray, Lord of Dunmore, lost control of the province and abandoned Williamsburg for a British ship anchored off of Yorktown. Sending out a call for loyal followers, Dunmore, obviously, hoped to return to the Governor's Palace in short order. In the end, he would be unsuccessful.

While the bulk of concerns seemed to rest on the coast in 1775, the western frontier was inevitably concerned about the potential for another series of attacks by Native Americans – but as opposed to years past, this time encouraged by the English. The fears would prove to be well founded at various places along the frontier, but not in the Shenandoah Valley.

This may have been the reason for Rader's Company being in Fort Pitt by October 1775. According to the only known morning report for Rader's Company, the company was near Fort Pitt at that time.

Once known as Fort Duquesne, the fort was a highly sought prize during the French and Indian War. At the time of the American Revolution, it continued to hold strong importance for the defense of people on the western frontier.

It is likely that Rader's company did not remain to long at Pitt and returned as a ready defense force for the central Valley. According to the *Historical Register of Virginians in the Revolution*, Rader was still in command of Virginia Militia as a captain in 1777. John Wayland found Rader's career extended into 1778, when he was listed as a major.

While the war progressed from 1775, there appears to have been a small number of men from the company that went on to serve with various regiments of the Virginia Continental Line. Some may have remained with the militia, but terms of enlistment usually ran for short periods of time – never have I seen one to run for the term of the war. It is likely that most, after having served their terms, returned to their farms and provided to the Patriotic cause with portions of their crops and livestock.

As for Rader himself, he was likely born in Augusta or Rockingham County, or even Bethlehem, Pennsylvania on March 8, 1750. The son of Adam and Margaret Maria Zimmerman Rader, Michael was descended from German-Swiss ancestry. Hans Adam Roder, Sr. was born in Bern, Switzerland about 1645. His namesake son was also born about 1668, also in Switzerland, but had moved to Mutterstadt, Germany where he died in 1720. His son, also with the same name, was born in 1706 and was the immigrant. Marrying Anna Barbara Bender (the daughter of Matthiaus), Captain Rader, through this, his grandmother. Captain Rader's father, Adam, was born in Bethlehem, Pa. in 1727.

Michael Rader married Catherina Long prior to the Revolutionary War, on December 25, 1769. Living in the area between New Market and Timberville through, at least, the 1790s, Rader and his family later moved to Mason, Virginia where he died in 1830.

Henkel Press Served Early Page Residents
(1806 – 1870)
Article of 10/31/2002

A few weeks back I introduced the mention of the Henkel Press as a part of the Kite Family profile. Considering that a very large part of Page County's early settlers and residence were of Germanic or Swiss origin, and that many of the same families continued to speak the language and engage in the old world customs, I thought it only appropriate to elaborate on the impact of the Henkel Press.

The Henkel Press had its roots in the life of a young Ambrose Henkel, son of Rev. Paul Henkel. The Henkel family had settled in New Market ca. 1790. In 1802, at sixteen years of age, Ambrose set out from New Market for Hagerstown with the intent of learning the printer's trade from the famous almanac printer, John Gruber. Apparently, whether a legend of not, Henkel was involved early on in the apprenticeship in helping to finish the almanac while Mr. Gruber was ill. When Ambrose was asked what the weather would be like during one day in July, he jokingly replied that it would snow . . . and that was how the other apprentices had it printed. Mr. Gruber was understandably very angry with the young apprentice and promised him that if it did not snow on that day, he would lose his job. Legend has it that it was indeed a small flurry on that day, preserving Henkel's apprenticeship.

By 1806 Henkel had completed his apprenticeship and returned to his parent's house in New Market, along with a wagonload of materials to build his own press. Most of the wood was of hand-hewn mahogany and cottonwood. Within the frame sat a 21 X 26 inch slab of granite.

By October 1807 the first newspaper in German south of the Mason Dixon Line was released by Henkel. *The Virginia and New Market Popular Instructor and Weekly News* must have been well received by the many peoples of Germanic descent in the Shenandoah Valley. By 1811, Henkel had two religious booklets and a very popular *ABC Kinderbook* for children, illustrated with woodcuts from Henkel himself.

Ambrose sold the press to Solomon Henkel ca. 1816 and it continued to serve the peoples of Germanic descent throughout the area and beyond. Though there are some indications that Ambrose still had dealings with the business, he refocused his life toward the ministry. Ordained in 1824, Ambrose continued the work of his father, preaching mostly in German at the Reformed Lutheran Church in town. He later served with his assistant, Socrates Henkel, at Emmanuel Lutheran Church from 1854 to 1859. Ambrose died in January 1870 and was buried in the Emmanuel Lutheran Church Cemetery.

In the end, the Henkel Press was responsible for publishing more Lutheran material than any other pres in the country.

Early and Antebellum Page County

Travel

Revisiting the Turnpike System in Page County, Part 1 (1813 – 1848)

Article of 10/23/2003

In his *Short History of Page County*, Harry M. Strickler briefly discussed the turnpike system that existed before 1860 in Page County. Taking what Strickler gave and adding it to what is available in the Board of Public Works records at the Library of Virginia, one can find a very interesting and detailed history on several of the turnpike, but not all.

Little is known, for example on the old turnpike that ran through Milam Gap. Strickler indicates that as early as 1813 this pike was in place, and, during the Civil War, soldiers often traveled along the old but difficult grade (in military records often the turnpike that ran through Milam Gap was confused with the one that ran through Fisher's Gap and vice versa).

At least a year before the Milam Gap Turnpike was built, a somewhat operational road/turnpike was running from New Market to Thornton Gap. However, it appears that in March 1819 measures were being taken to improve the road through an act of the Virginia General Assembly. On March 4 of that year it had been noted that $15,000 in subscriptions had been made for the New Market Turnpike. Regretfully, once again, beyond that little is known about the turnpike as it came into development and, afterwards, its demise before the New Market to Sperryville was built in 1849.

The next system to run through Page, recorded with the Public Works Records, was supposed to have been the Harrisonburg & Thornton's Gap Turnpike Company. Though it is recorded as having been incorporated in 1831, there is no further information available on the system.

A third major turnpike in the Page Valley was established in 1839 with the Staunton to Luray Turnpike. This particular turnpike held great value later on as the Virginia Central Railroad later arrived in Staunton, giving an excellent outlet for Page Valley produced goods. Though it did not run the course of Rt. 340 in the Southern part of the county, it did begin near the present crossing of Rt. 340 on the Page/Rockingham County line but made an abrupt turn back toward the river, ran along the river and along Rt. 683 (what some locals remember as the old wagon road), generally rejoining the present intersection of 683 and Rt. 340. The turnpike continued somewhat along the present course of Rt. 340 North as far as Grove Hill and then took a right turn along what is known today as Rt. 650 or the Grove Hill River Road going all the way to Honeyville (where the turnpike would eventually merge with the Gordonsville Turnpike when it was later built) on to Alma and making a right turn (along Wampler Rd.) to the present Rt. 616/Leaksville Road to Luray. Heading South from the Verbena or Price's Mill, this old turnpike ran through Port Republic, Mt. Meridian, New Hope, and eventually across Christian Creek to Staunton.

In 1848 a major development came with the improvement of the old New Market Turnpike when the New Market to Sperryville Turnpike was incorporated. Apparently, the older incorporation came along with the old turnpike had folded for a period of time and, as the road went into disrepair, there was an obvious need to incorporate another turnpike company. Essentially, this turnpike somewhat followed the course of present Rt. 211 though there are many variances. One example of the difference between present Rt. 211 and the old Sperryville Turnpike is the present Hamburg Road, an original part of the old turnpike grade that ran next to the stage stop, Calendine, and the Mauck Meeting House.

Revisiting the Turnpike System in Page County, Part 2 (1848 – 1858) Article of 11/13/2003

Perhaps the best-documented incorporations to come to Page County was with the Blue Ridge Turnpike Company that actually was the authority over the New Market to Gordonsville Turnpike. Though the incorporation was given in 1848, the company came into existence as an organization in 1850. A great reason behind the incorporation of this turnpike was obvious simply through the design in the seal showing the sheaves of wheat. In the early development and minutes of the organization the turnpike would serve central Page Valley commerce most reasonably through a very good access to markets on the eastern side of the Blue Ridge. Paschal Graves was one of the forerunners of the organization and was the first President and was succeeded by the mid-1850s by Frank Jordan.

A wonderful turnpike, it technically began near the point of the present Rt.340/Rt. 340 By-Pass near New Market Gap, actually intersecting with the New Market-Sperryville Turnpike. From there, it ran a course in the general area of Battle Creek and turned off along what is now known as Rt. 614/Shuler Lane (where you begin to get an excellent feel of how the turnpike actually looked, excepting the gravel along the road now) to Columbia Bridge, which was a part of the turnpike.

According to the Public Works records, this amazing bridge consisted of two spans of 145 feet each with lattice and arch. At a cost of a whopping $277,000 not only was the bridge a rather pricey feature of the turnpike; it was also amazing in construction. On September 30, 1851, Engineer James Anthony wrote "The Shenandoah Bridge necessarily a costly work from its style and magnitude is rendered still more so by over caution in having very thick walls in the abutments. It is however a superior structure."

Continuing on from the bridge, the turnpike ran toward Honeyville, thereby intersecting with the Luray to Staunton Turnpike for a short length of about a mile, then took the course of the present Honeyville Road (not through the present town of Stanley, but winding around a bit and eventually, likely, linking with the present Judy Lane and then onto Rt. 611/Chapel Road). Here it passed by Graves' Chapel and extended on toward the present Red Gate Road and up a very winding road to Franklin Cliffs and Fishers Gap.

Finally another very necessary road was incorporated in 1851 with the Luray to Front Royal Turnpike Company. Obviously, this extended Page County's mercantile trade along a northern corridor to larger markets and toward another significant railroad outlet. Essentially, it ran along the length of present Rt. 340 from Luray to Front Royal, but jumped about a bit, left and right of the present road. This road had a series of bridges but was of a much smaller scale of those along the South Fork of the Shenandoah (the Columbia [1851], White House [ca. 1850] and Red Bridge [ca. 1850]), needing only to cross along creeks.

Though incorporated in 1858, very little is revealed in the state records as to the details behind the Luray and Hardy Turnpike Company. As Harry M. Strickler mentions, this road ran along Bixlers Ferry Road to "Caroline Furnace and on westward."

In-depth research of the Public Works Records can yield much more beyond the information I've presented in this and the previous article including extensive lists of stockholders, certificates of stocks, letters, engineer and board reports and even maps.

Comparing Modern Travel with 19th Century Travel – A Glimpse at the Differences (1840s – 1850s) Article of 8/19/2004

In this modern age of travel, we can easily take for granted the fact that we can now make in a matter of hours what once may have been a journey of several days. Additionally, travel by automobile is indeed much more luxurious now than before – with our comfortable seats, radios, and even built-in DVD players for some. In his *Ups and Downs of a Confederate Soldier*, once again, James Huffman's recollections of life during the mid-1800s (before the Civil War) prove interesting reading in comparing modern travel with that of nearly 150 years ago.

Perhaps his earliest recollections of any long trip, Huffman first recounted the events that surrounded his family's move from Alma to Naked Creek. He recalled that the family moved using a wagon and that the "train was well fitted with household goods, leaving a small space well nigh the bows where a commodious chafftick was spread for the comfort of several of the smallest of us . . . After a full day's travel on this slow train we arrived at our new home with no serious accident."

Huffman also remembered of the years after settling at the new homestead on Naked Creek that the family had an "extra-good team of four horses and a knock-about team. The best team was well harnessed and equipped. The leaders had twelve-inch back bands and everything in proportion, with double-link homemade traces and chains, so close and tight that one could hold them out like a whip. The wheel horses had six-inch breeching, with the other parts of the harness in proportion – tight double – link traces and a large ornamented iron wagon, painted beautifully and striped, with bed so high that one could walk straight under the bows; two good sheets to make it dry inside in all kinds of weather; a side box for curry comb and brush, axe and Jackscrew, inside a tar bucket dangling on the coupling pole behind. A feed trough was hung against the hindgate, with a half-bushel; cedar bucket tied in the trough, and a provision box with division box fitted for half-moon pies, coffee and sugar bags. The latter we always had refilled gratis by the merchant who bought the load."

When he was "about fourteen"(1854), Huffman remembered was beginning to "feel very mannish and begged my father to let me drive this team. When he consented, I felt considerably bigger than President Taft or any other that ever occupied the President's chair." While it may have taken a good days travel for a full family in a filled wagon from Alma to Naked Creek, more distant travels took considerably more time. Recalled Huffman, "if no trouble occurred, it required four days to go to Gordonsville, four to Orange Courthouse, six to Winchester and eight to Fredericksburg."

While we concern ourselves with the possibility of a flat tire or engine trouble, in the 1850s the obvious concerns weren't too far removed from those of modern times in that then they were the wheels and the horses. "The thing I feared most on these long trips when I was so young," recalled Huffman, "was a sick horse. I had a large saddle horse that often was ailing and I would stick something in his mouth until he quit grunting. I thought sometimes he quit to get rid of the nuisance."

Other problems more particular to earlier times was either the washout of a road, or even worse, the loss of a bridge during travels. James had a few harrowing tales to share in his book about his travels to Winchester and across the Blue Ridge to Fredericksburg, but one he mentioned gave indication to the first loss of the old White House Bridge, in the mid-1850s. Though he did not witness the event personally, he did convey the story that "the wind lifted the White house three-span bridge from the piers and turned it over in the river with a team of horses on it."

Since the Huffman family also ran a large sawmill at their farm on Naked Creek, James also recalled traveling by flatboat on the Shenandoah River – a topic that will be covered in an upcoming article.

Slavery

Slavery and the early break-ups of Baptists Congregations in Page County (1800 – 1840s) Article of 5/27/2004

Sometime following 1800, there began a series of disagreements within the Mill Creek Baptist congregation over the practice of slavery. According to Harry M. Strickler's *Short History of Page County*, the one dissenting group "refused to correspond with churches that permitted their members to hold slaves." Some believe that, though converted Baptists, many members held onto Mennonite ways of thought in that, as a matter of an article of faith, the church should not hold with slavery, the bearing of arms or the taking of legal oaths." Elder John Koontz held that these things were matters for individual conscience and should not be a part of church doctrine.

However, eventually a portion of the congregation broke-off and began holding worship services at the White House, just west of Hamburg. Following the death of Martin Coffman. Jr. in 1805, Martin Kaufman III, Lewis Seitz, and Samuel Comer officially separated from the Mill Creek Church with a group of fifteen followers (six families) and moved to Fairfield County, Ohio.

The move was an ideal situation for those with anti-slavery sentiment in that, under the Ordinance of 1787, slavery had been prohibited north of the Ohio River. Additionally, following the Battle of Fallen Timbers in 1794, and after the Treaty of Greenville in 1796, settlement in that area had finally become relatively safe. At the time of the move to Ohio, Fairfield County was only five years old and had been only the eighth county to be formed in the Northwest Territory.

Once in Ohio, the former members of the Mill Creek congregation established the Pleasant Run Baptist Church in Lancaster. The church was first constituted in 1806 and, on April 19th of that same year, the new congregation met "according to appointment and opened our meeting with prayer and praise. Second – proceeded to business, with choosing our Moderator, Martin Coffman. We ended our meeting with praise and thanksgiving." In that same year, the Pleasant Run Church also issued a statement making clear their views on slavery. "We do not wish to correspond with any association or church that does in principle or practice hold involuntary slavery."

By 1809, the congregation had nearly 80 members and was one of four churches to become a part of the Scioto Baptists Association (named for the nearby Scioto River).

Various surnames of the membership are reflective of surnames which have been are prevalent in the history of Page County since the 1700s, including Beaver, Coffman, Comer, Geiger, Hiestand, Hite, Huffman, Pence, Ruffner, and Spitler.

The "break of 1805" would not be the last time that slavery would come into play in the Baptist Church in Page County. In the 1840s, Page County Baptists were effected by a nationwide rift that ended up creating what was known as New School or Missionary Baptists (the division actually happened as early as 1837 in Ohio). As Harry Strickler points out, other churches were also affected by the subject of slavery, resulting in a rift in the Presbyterian Church at nearly the same time; the Lutheran Church in the 1850s and the Methodist Church at the onset of the American Civil War.

Westward Ventures: James T. Marye and a Letter to a Friend, Part 1
(1843)
Article of 1/30/2003

Now and then, a document that drifts from within the borders of Page County eventually finds its way home. Indeed, as luck would have it, I recently had the opportunity to acquire a document relating to an early aspect of Page history and an early Page family.

As the Marye family has been fairly well covered here and there in the annals of Page County history, this particular document, a letter from 1843, reveals a little about one James Theodosius Marye, a son of William Staige and Elizabeth Ruffner Marye. Named for an uncle, James was born on December 9, 1814. Around the age of 20, James T. Marye ventured out with dreams of wealth and prosperity in Mississippi.

On December 20, 1835, James wrote his friend (and perhaps former employer) in Luray, Reuben P. Bell, of his exploits to date. "I landed at this place on the 8th Oct. after some forty days out from home" wrote James, "but was not all the time traveling." From Virginia, James had made his way through Kanawha County to Kentucky and thence to Louisville, from which he took passage "down the Ohio and Mississippi Rivers" which was "gratifying indeed although I was detained some 10 days on the way in consequence of low water longer than is usually taken performing the passage."

Upon arriving at Port Gibson, James found gainful employment as a clerk at a "large Mercantile House" that sold "upwards of 100 thousand dollars worth of goods per annum." "I have to attend the desk from morning till 10 o'clock at night, writing. It is the custom of this county to have his account on the first of January, when his account when his account is considered due, and if he does not pay it he gives his note and pays 10 per ct. or payable and negotiable in Bank."

James made emphasis for his old friend to come and join him. "Bell, I think this is the very county for you. I will venture you can make more here in 1 year than you can in Page in 4." Of course, the times and the profit of slave labor fueled James' enthusiasm.

". . . you could come here with 10 hands at least, and be able to buy you a Plantation and go to work. With your 10 hands you could produce 70 bales of cotton at 70 cents per bale would be 49.00 $ besides the opportunity of speculating in land and the increase of your property."

"All kinds of business is better here than it is in Va." wrote James, "Planters get rich, lawyers, doctors, Merchants, mechanics, tailors, sailors, overseers, and all kinds of men have made a fortune here in the last five years. The Gentleman with whom I am living sold a plantation on yesterday for 130 Thousand Dollars to a man who commanded the world by overseeing not 10 years ago."

Westward Ventures: James T. Marye and a Letter to a Friend, Part 2 (1843) Article of 2/13/2003

In continuing an examination of James T. Marye's December 20, 1835 letter to Reuben P. Bell, we recall his enthusiasm for the life that he had found at Port Gibson, Mississippi. However, with the wealth and prosperity of the area came a price. James continued . . .

"Living is devilish high. I am paying 240$ a year for board (More money than I was in Va. for my services). Washing will cost me 25 or 30$ more, but taking all these high charges into consideration I shall make more this year than I have made in all my life before, and don't work half as hard as I formally have done."

Before he closed his enthusiastic letter, James also relayed a little color of the locality, "The weather is quite warm, the Thermometer ranges from 60 to 70 degrees. The grass is green as spring. The roses are in full bloom. We have plenty of rain, (and) the cotton crop will not be so abundant in consequence of it. I find a great abundance of Virginians here & indeed you will find men from all parts of U.S. and coming forth to secure a part of the bounty. Many are coming off from Alabama finding this to be a place of more profit."

Interestingly, James made no mention of a wife, Elizabeth Bush, to whom, according to genealogical records, he was married on March 5, 1834. Elizabeth may have died early in marriage as James later married Mary Passmore Hoopes (born the daughter of Passmore and Eliza T. Moore Hoopes in West Chester, Pennsylvania in 1820). James and Mary Marye had at least nine children. One daughter, Maddie May, later married first cousin William Augustus Marye in Nevada in 1879.

James T. Marye died on August 10, 1867 and was buried in Winter Green Cemetery, Port Gibson, Mississippi.

James' friend and perhaps former employer, Reuben P. Bell did not take James' advice and remove himself from Page County for Mississippi. In 1860, Reuben was listed as living in the Hope Mills area at age 52 and quite a rather wealthy farmer with $12,000 in Real Estate. A slaveholder since the 1830s, Reuben may have been somewhat interested in James' referrals to the profit of slavery at Port Gibson, but were not enough to encourage his relocation to Mississippi. However, Reuben's life went much farther than farming as he was known, among other things, as a member of Page County's school commissioners in 1846, the 25th Justice of Page County in the 1850s, a commissioner of the Luray Valley Railroad Company in 1870, and a judge of election appointed by the court in 1870 for Springfield. Reuben died in Page County on April 24, 1876 and was buried in Green Hill Cemetery. While he remained in the county, some of his children did in fact end up in points west of Virginia.

Dr. Henry Ruffner and His Famous Abolition Pamphlet, Part 1
(1790 – 1847)
Article of 1/8/2004

In his *Short History of Page County*, author and county historian Harry M. Strickler touched briefly on the life of Dr. Henry Ruffner but did not mention much of the famous pamphlet that Ruffner released in 1847.

Born in Mundellsville (in the locale of Willow Grove Mill) in Page County, on January 16, 1790, Henry Ruffner was the oldest son of Col. David and Ann Brumback Ruffner. By the time young Henry was six years old, Col. David Ruffner and his family moved to the Kanawha Valley where Joseph, David's father, had already relocated a year before. Therefore, Henry's life in northern Page (then Shenandoah County), likely had little to no major impact, one way or the other, on his outlook on the politics of slavery later in his life.

While laboring on his father's farm and salt works just below Malden, Virginia (now West Virginia), Henry Ruffner initially received a common education. However, according to one biographical sketch, "When near 20 years of age, his father observing his love for literature and fondness for books, [and] sent him to an Academy at Lewisburg, Greenbrier County." Ran by Presbyterian minister Rev. Dr. McElheny, the Academy was a major influence on Ruffner's life and choice for future religious practice. Joining the Presbyterian Church, Ruffner eventually expressed a desire to enter the ministry. After graduating from Washington College in 1814, Ruffner spent several years in the study of divinity, in 1819 he was licensed by the presbytery. Though Ruffner headed several pastorates in Rockbridge County, he also took time to found one near his family's salt works in Kanawha Valley in 1830. Henry, however, was not limited to preaching as he also found work as a professor at his alma mater, eventually becoming president of the institution in 1837. A year later, Princeton University conferred upon Ruffner the degree of D.D.

As if his practice and profession did not keep him occupied, for several years Ruffner took time to author a number of works including *A Discourse upon the Duration of Future Punishment* (Richmond, 1823): *Inaugural Address* (Lexington, 1837); and *Judith Bensaddi, a Romance* (1840). Ruffner also took interest in publishing a number of discourses against slavery, including his most famous *An Address to the People of West Virginia* (Lexington, Va.) in 1847. The publication actually came about as a result of the presentation that Ruffner had made to the Franklin Society in August 1847. In a letter to Ruffner dated September 1, 1847, several notable personalities of Virginia history (among whom were included former Gov. S. McDowell Moore, future Gov. John Letcher, and John Echols) had actually "petitioned" Ruffner to publish his address.

In its subtitle, the address made clear that slavery was "injurious to the public welfare, and that it may be gradually abolished without detriment to the rights and interests of slaveholders." However, if one takes time to read carefully and understand the nature of Ruffner's approach, by no means did his argument ring in tune with the nature of the more famous Northern abolitionists.

Dr. Henry Ruffner and his Famous Abolition Pamphlet, Part 2 (1847 – 1861) 1/22/2004

Through his famous pamphlet, Page County-born Dr. Henry Ruffner, (a slaveholder himself) worked on the agenda of economic and political ramifications of slavery rather than moral arguments against the institution. At first appearance, it might seem that Ruffner, influenced by his life while a youth in the Kanawha Valley and after that as a resident of Rockbridge County, by 1847, appeared to offer a solution. However, upon examination of the actual pamphlet, Ruffner held a great deal of contempt toward slaves and spoke of them in none other than derogatory terms.

From the outset, Ruffner's beliefs clearly stated that the institution of slavery had not been as successful in the western portion of the state as it had in the eastern portion and had done nothing more than harm the area through economics and by discouraging immigrants from settling in the region. With that in mind, Ruffner supported abolition as a way to free whites, not blacks, from slavery. Not only did he feel that the institution deterred immigrants but also influenced an exodus of sorts, arguing that slavery was to be attributed to the fact that the Commonwealth had probably lost by emigration 300,000 more persons than all of the old free states.

"She has sent—or we should rather say, she has driven from her soil—at least one third of all the emigrants, who have gone from the old States to the new. More than another third have gone from the other old slave states . . .. These were generally industrious and enterprising white men, who found by sad experience, that a country of slaves was not the country for them. It is a truth, a certain truth, that slavery drives free laborers, — farmers, mechanics, and all, and some of the best of them too — out of the country"

As a solution, Ruffner, using the Great Valley of Virginia, which he considered from Montgomery County north to the Potomac, as the primary platform of action and proposed a gradual and complete emancipation in Virginia. After freeing the slaves, Ruffner also proposed a program of colonization or deportation of the former slaves to Liberia, working into an earlier established idea spearheaded much earlier by President James Monroe. Joining with his father in the argument, with his publication of a sermon he made in Philadelphia in 1852, William Henry Ruffner (Washington College, 1842) saw this as an opportunity as favorable mostly because of its "missionary aspects" and proposed a program of education before re-colonizing them in Liberia.

While the complexities behind emancipation and colonization were vast, Ruffner's argument boiled down to the fact that once the slaves were gone, white's could again have opportunity to find jobs that were otherwise being consumed by the use of slave labor.

Ultimately, it appears that a good deal of support for Ruffner's argument came from several of those counties west of the Blue Ridge while the more politically dominant and influential eastern section of the state denounced such actions. Though an attempt was made in 1857 to test Ruffner's theory in Wayne County, Virginia (now West Virginia), the experiment failed because of the inability of some investors to contribute and the fact that a national economic depression had come along.

While the mention of Ruffner's pamphlet had become relatively "unmentionable" not long after its publication, it would again come into play and bear an interesting impact in the 1859 Virginia gubernatorial election. A brief discussion of this follows next week in the conclusion.

The Ruffner Pamphlet and the 1859 Virginia Governor's Race (1859)
Article of 1/29/2004

In a small portion of the book *The Secession Movement in Virginia* (1934), Professor Henry T. Shanks brought attention to the role of the Ruffner Pamphlet in the 1859 Virginia Governor's race.

During the Democratic nomination run-off, John Letcher (one who endorsed the Ruffner Pamphlet in 1847) may have regretted his stand just over a decade before. There was an intricate web of politics involved, but essentially, because of his 1847 actions in respect to the pamphlet, Letcher had to contend with several political attacks from the Whig party as well as some rather radical elements of the Democratic party. For his actions in respect to the pamphlet, Letcher was labeled by most of his enemy's as being "unsound" on the issue of slavery.

In his own defense, and to gain the support of the "Southern Rights Democrats," Letcher quickly spoke out that Ruffner had actually changed his address from his oral presentation of "a calm argument on the social and political influence of slavery upon agricultural and mechanical development of Western Virginia" to one in the pamphlet that "contained many things so exceptional that those . . . who called upon him to publish his speech refused to contribute to the cost of the publication of the pamphlet."

Furthermore, Letcher claimed that his own views had changed considerably since 1847. Originally, he claimed that he believed that slavery was a political and social evil but was not one to be considered a moral evil. He showed proof of this in that he had owned slaves since 1847 as a matter of purchase and not one of inheritance. Additionally, he claimed that the abolitionists' attacks had given him sufficient time to reflect and to come to the conclusion that his former views on political and social evils of the institution were wrong. This satisfied the radical arm of the media but the more radical eastern planter element was still not content and continued a campaign against him.

Despite it all, and with the fact that the democrats brought five candidates to the party's nomination convention (helping to split the vote even more), Letcher won the nomination with 16,115 votes more than the other candidates.

When it came down to Letcher's run against Whig W.L. Goggin for the governor's office, the pamphlet again played a role and may have cost him votes in the east, yet securing more votes in the west (including Page County).

Inevitably, Virginia's 1859 decision to go with Letcher may have gained the Commonwealth time and a significant amount of patience when it came to actions toward secession in 1861. A strong Union man, Letcher tried several measures to avoid war, including playing an instrumental role in the Peace Conference of February 1861 (at the end of the Buchanan administration) as well as sending a number of representatives to see Lincoln in person within two months of his inauguration. However, "coercion" by the Federal government was the one item that Virginia would not give on and, when Lincoln made the call for 75,000 troops, the scales were tipped for secession to finally bring the Commonwealth into the Confederacy.

Ironically, Henry Ruffner, after being able to bear witness to all that built up the war, died on December 17, 1861. Regretfully, he left no written words on his views of the war or in regard to the impact that his pamphlet had on pre-war Virginia politics.

Frank Veney – The Other Half of the Bethany Veney Story (1850s – 1915) Article of 7/1/2004

In April 1915, the *Page News & Courier* featured a story about Frank Veney, stating that he claimed to be over one hundred and twelve years old at the time. Though he was, according to census records, more than likely born around 1830 rather than 1803, in his remarkable life span, Veney made the claim of having been married no less than 25 times. The paper read, "Whether his claim of having lived more than a century can be substantiated, the old man bears unmistakable marks of having weathered a long and checkered career. All this is evidenced by his flowing gray locks, his palsied form and unsteady gait. All this coupled with his great memory of the stirring incidents recorded by ancient history and we find the elements that contribute to perhaps the oldest person in Page County."

Though he claimed to have been married twenty-five times, Veney, in his March 30, 1915 interview, could only recall the names of eleven of his wives. Interestingly, Frank Veney can be found in the 1860 Page County census records as being a free man, 30 years of age and living with his son, Joshua (12) at the William H. Brumback place in Luray. Though he was free, many of the wives that Veney could recollect had been slaves. To the best of his memory, his first wife was "Nancy." Though he could not recall the first name of the next wife, he did remember that her last name was "Mullen." Veney could not remember his third wife's name whatsoever but did recall that she had been a slave and was owned by a man by the name of Mills in Greene County. The fourth wife recalled was Fannie Brady, "who died after being married on year leaving an infant child" (perhaps Joshua). "On her dying bed the woman requested as her last wish that Frank marry her sister, Mary, in order that the child should be taken care of. Frank Veney married her as his fifth wife, and then followed by Sarah Smith. However, that "domestic felicity was of short duration" as he had "found out some things on her that made him leave her." Frank Veney's next marriage was to Mildred Todd, and then a "woman by the name of "Read." Finally, by the mid 1850s (according to how Bethany Veney's account reads), it appears that he finally married Bethany. Bethany was at that time a slave belonging to John Printz.

According to Frank, "She was a noted cook employed by the late Daniel Adams (likely this was G.J. Adams) who conducted a hotel for many years in Luray. Before being in the employ of the Adams hotel she was bought by the late David McKay of Luray. She did a great deal of the cooking for the hands of Mr. McKay while he as engaged in building a railroad (actually a turnpike) in Bath County."

Though standing in stark contrast with the story that appears in Bethany Veney's personal account *The Narrative of Bethany Veney: A Slave Woman*, published in 1889) and reasoning for leaving Page County in 1858, Frank Veney recalled "Influenced that she possessed in the culinary art finally led to her settling in Worcester, Massachusetts, where she now lives at One hundred and three years of age."

Frank Veney continued that "After leaving these parts Frank Veney says he never heard anything of her whereabouts for three year, and thinking she was dead, the old man made another matrimonial plunge" with his next wife, Mandy or Amanda Jeffries. To this particular marriage was born a daughter, Flora (ca. 1874), who later married Cyrus Dixon in 1902. It is with Flora Dixon that Frank Veney resided at the time of the interview, "in the western suburbs" of Luray.

Interestingly, Frank Veney stated at the end of his interview that he had been in "correspondence with his former wife in Massachusetts, who has made many contributions to his comfort in his declining years."

Contrary Viewpoints on the "Peculiar Institution" and Secession in Page County (1861)

Article of 5/20/2004

A recent finding in a mid-1900's issue of the *Page News & Courier* has revealed evidence that would suggest that, in 1860/61, at least two Page County slaveholders were not a party to "driving public opinion toward the Confederate cause," leaving question as to just how many more Page County slaveholders were opposed to Virginia's secession and may have agreed more with the ideas delivered years before in the famous Ruffner Pamphlet.

Recounting "early days," Isaac Shuler (1849-1942), a son of John (1815 – 1908) and Mary Kite Shuler (1820-1897), remembered the two opposing parties over the matter of secession in Page. However, he also recalled that his father, John Shuler, and John Lionberger, spoke out against secession as a hasty and unnecessary act. "Naturally there were speeches on both sides," wrote Isaac Shuler. "John Lionberger, Dr. Galipio, R.M. Walton and John Shuler spoke in opposition to it, and portrayed what the results would be if the State of Virginia seceded." While John Shuler (a 45 year-old farmer residing in Grove Hill District #1 with $6,375 in personal property) had owned two slaves in 1840 (1) and 1850 (2), by 1860 he had either emancipated or sold them. Additionally, despite his stand against secession, John Lionberger, a prominent 52 year-old "Gentlemen" (with over $24,000 in personal property) of Luray, owned as many as fourteen slaves by 1860, having increased his "slaveholdings" significantly since 1840. While a "Dr. Galipio cannot be found in Page County records, Reuben M. Walton was a 42 year-old merchant in Newport and owned no slaves between 1840 and 1860.

Isaac Shuler continued, "On one occasion which I will never forget, they were speaking at R.M. Walton's store at Newport. Mr. Lionberger was speaking when the crowds yelled for Squire John Shuler. He responded and in his discourse followed along the line of Lionberger, trying to impress upon the minds of his hearers the horror and bloodshed that would follow secession."

"During his remarks there was a man in the audience who took an exception and made for the speaker. He dropped back in the store and grabbed a chair. R.M. Walton jumped to the counter and prevented the blow. The crowd not satisfied yelled for Shuler to again take up the speech and in his remarks said something that was displeasing to some present. They said, if we cannot get out rights in Virginia we will go to South Carolina, if we have to wade in blood up to our knees. The speaker had great respect for them and said you need not to go South Carolina where you can get all the fight in Virginia, and probably near your home."

Shuler also recalled of the man who spoke out regarding his desires to move to South Carolina . . . "did he fight!? – no he kept out of it." Of those who spoke out against secession, neither fought as they were beyond the age of service. Reuben M. Walton was also overage but later, in 1864, served in the 8th Battalion Virginia Reserves. Despite Shuler and Lionberger's not fighting, they both contributed sons to the Confederate service. John Shuler's son, Michael Shuler, later served in Co. H, 33rd Virginia Infantry, was elected to captain in the spring of 1862 and was killed at the Battle of the Wilderness on May 5, 1864. Shuler's daughter, Emma Jane, was also betrothed to Sgt. Isaac Newton Koontz when he was executed after the war at Rude's Hill.

John Lionberger's son, John Henry Lionberger, a student at the Virginia Military Institute at the opening of the war, began his service as a drillmaster and then left the Corps of Cadets to serve with the Dixie Artillery. Elected 1st lieutenant with Co. D, 7th Virginia Cavalry, Lionberger later resigned and secured a lieutenancy with Co. C, 39th Battalion Virginia Cavalry (Gen. R.E. Lee's Couriers and Bodyguards) with which unit he served until the close of the war.

Early Life

A 1905 interview with John P. Louderback (1850s) Article of 7/8/2004

Born February 8, 1836 in Page County, John Philip Louderback was the oldest son of Isaac and Elizabeth Foltz Louderback. By profession his father was a millwright residing in Alma District 1 in 1860 with $315 in real estate. However, unlike his father, John took on the occupation of shoemaker with which he was engaged in 1860, at the age of 24, while still residing with his parents. One of a number of Page County men to enlist in Co. I (as opposed to Co. K), 10th Virginia Infantry, Louderback endured over three years of war before being captured at the Battle of Fisher's Hill in September 1864. Surviving the hardships of prisoner of war camp, Louderback returned to Page County and enjoyed a long and successful life. Louderback married Sarah Ellen Modesitt (daughter of Charles B. & Elizabeth Kibler Modesitt) on October 14, 1875.

As luck would have it, old copies of the newspaper give a rare peak at early life in Page County through the eyes of John P. Louderback. A resident of Newport at the time, Louderback dropped by the newspaper office and related some "personal recollections extending back 20 years prior to the war." In his interview, he remembered a time when there "were only three houses between his home and Shenandoah City – not there are thirty to forty . . . the closest store was at Honeyville and was a branch store conducted by Jordan of Luray. The great place in those days to buy goods was New Market. His father frequently went to that place with a few dozen eggs which he traded for groceries at Henkel's store at 4 and 6 cents a dozen. These trips were made on foot, people seldom rode in those days. Reuben Foltz (1782-1869), the Newport miller, would boat 75 to 100 barrels of flour down the Shenandoah and Potomac to Washington and Alexandria, sell the flour at $3.00 a barrel and return all the way on foot with the money in his pocket, the boatmen accompanying him for protection."

Louderback also recalled the thriftiness of Page residents stating "the good old people of Page were nothing if not economical. They wagoned to Fredericksburg and traded produce for a year's supply of various provisions – and the quantities they brought back with them would keep a family but a few weeks now. Twenty-five to fifty pounds of sugar was a year's supply. Mr. Louderback says his earliest recollection is of coffee just once a week and that on Sunday morning. The young ladies went to church barefooted with their shoes wrapped up under their arm. If young men went home with them they would put on their shoes . . . [thereby] they saved sole leather. Every body worse home spun of course, and a boy was just as proud as a new suit as now. While economy was the rule of the day people had abundance to eat and lived comfortably. Cooking stoves were unknown and all culinary operations went on over the fire place. Whiskey was cheap and abundant. Distiller Kite always knocked the head out of a barrel when he wanted the election to go his way and the thirsty voters crowded around to drink out of tin cups. Everybody was a Democrat in those days. Wheat brought from 75 cents to $1.00 a bushel. There were no large farmers and few put in more than 5 or 10 acres of what. Mr. Louderback can remember only three in his end of Page who famed extensively. This was mainly because of primitive modes of tilling the land." Louderback also remembered the days when both English and German were spoken in Page County. It was not uncommon as German was the mother tongue of many who had settled in the area years before (some as early as the 1720s) and, due to the isolated nature of the Page Valley, it remained dominant in use locally through the middle to latter 19th century in the schools and in churches (Lutheran and Brethren in particular).

John P. Louderback lived until 1919, outliving his wife by just five years. Both are buried at Graves Chapel Cemetery in Stanley.

Page County Recollections: Processing Flax and Wool in the 19th Century, Part 1 (1840s – 1850s) Article of 7/22/2004

Regretfully, over time, recollections of the way things were done in the old days have passed from memory. Much knowledge has been lost simply because the old ways, as passed along by word of mouth, were not passed down to succeeding generations either because the next generation didn't really care to hear or the preceding generation didn't think it was important to pass along. However, there are those who have taken the time to tell a story to those who would listen, and they, in turn, take the time to transcribe that information for generations to come.

One old way of the farm that can still be recounted by a few was the way fax and wool was turned into clothing. Despite the fact that Page did have woolen mills nearby, many locals still made their own cloth at home.

Though I have brought up James Huffman's book *Ups and Downs of a Confederate Soldier* (1940) a few years ago, I believe that the book is of much greater value for its materials discussing life before than during the Civil War. Speaking from the memory from his childhood, Huffman painted a very clear and vivid picture as to how life was on his parent's [Ambrose (1804-1862) and Christina Strole Huffman (1808-1893)] farm on the Page County side of Naked Creek between 1845 and 1860.

"At the proper season, we prepared a piece of ground for flax and sowed it. When in bloom it was beautiful to look over, being solid blue. When ripe, we pulled it, tied it in little bundles, shocked it up and when dry, beat the seed off. We then spread it on the ground in swathes (like wheat spread with a cradle) until well-rotted and black; then gathered it and broke it on a flax brake made of large, wooden blades, by holding a handful in the left hand in the brake and working the brake head with the right hand – up and down – chopping the wooden blades together until the stalk was broken into bits. We used only the bark or lint. Then it was ready for the scutcher. This was done by having an upright (a board) either fastened on a block or driven in the ground, at a height that would permit one to stand erect and grasp a handful in the middle, holding it on the board. Then with an oak paddle, eighteen or twenty inches long with both edges nicely sharpened to the point (the scutcher), the flax was beaten until soft and all the beards knocked out. Next, it was hackled by being drawn through a hatchel made of about a hundred sharp, slender, needle-like teeth, four or five inches long fastened in a stout board. Now it was ready for the spinning wheel. The combings of the hackle are as the combings of a woman's hair and are called tow." (thus the origin of the phrase "tow head) when referring to persons with blonde hair).

"Spinning was done in late fall or winter – mostly at night by pine-fire light from the fireplace. Tallow candles furnished the only other lights we had in those days, and if you will extinguish all lights and set a lighted candle in your room, you can tell how brilliant it is. My mother usually spun the straight flax and my sisters, the tow."

I imagine I can almost hear mother's voice singing softly to the hum of the flyer, interrupted by 'Get out of my light!' or 'Put on a piece of pine.' This flax was spun very fine or coarse, as desired, and with remarkable uniformity by the old expert spinners. Very fine sewing thread was made. This was prepared and woven into the finest linen cloth for shirts, trousers, tablecloths, towels and all kinds of linen apparel used in that day and time. The size of the flax thread is made altogether with the fingers. I could spin tow on the little wheel and woolen rolls on the big wheel."

Huffman's recollections of processing wool in the mid-19th century will follow next week.

Page County Recollections: Processing Flax and Wool in the 19th Century, Part 2 (1840s – 1850s) Article of 7/29/2004

While Huffman's recollections concluded last week with the processing of flax, his recollections of the way wool was processed are just as interesting. Keep in mind that Huffman was recalling the way things were done on his family's farm on Naked Creek between 1845 and 1860. Additionally, to better give an idea of the setting, Huffman recalled that the farm was quite large. In addition to a "good-sized brick house," the family had "a good barn, lumber mill, merchandise and chopping mill, store, tan-yard, blacksmith shop, ice house and other farm buildings such as a meat house, corn house, loom house, hen house and more than three hundred acres of land in the home tract and three or four hundred more in other tracts." Additionally, with all of the work required on such a large farm, Ambrose Huffman used his children (ten were born between 1833 and 1854 – six children were born at the old family farm near Alma and four at the farm on Naked Creek) as a main source of labor along with some local hired laborers, owning no slaves and not actually having a slave working for him until 1860 – having leased one (according to the 1860 slave census schedules) from Ambrose C. Booton (who lived at Leaksville).

Huffman recalled that he was even amazed at how efficient the farm was in meeting the needs of a large family. "Remember we were producing almost our entire living right on the farm without going off for anything. We did not raise coffee or sugar, yet there were substitutes, even for coffee and sugar. All kinds of grain and cloth, and clothing, from head to foot, were produced right from the soil on the farm and manufactured right at home, not shoddy and cheap, but good, substantial, nice and respectable goods."

Of the wool process, Huffman wrote, "To make woolen cloth, we had a flock of sheep that we sheared in the spring. Wool was washed clean, dried, and everything picked out that would not wash out. The nap was opened, put in bed sheets which were pinned with thorns gathered from thorn bushes, then taken to a carding machine where it was carded into rolls. Then it was brought home and spun on the big wheel into yarn, relled into hanks, sometimes doubled and twisted, and prepared for all kinds of woolen cloth for men's clothing, and beautiful, striped cloth or plain linsey for women and children. I can remember yet some of the striped linsey dresses that I wore when four to six years old."

"All socks and stockings were knit by our mothers and sisters, mostly at night, from yarn spun by their own hands. Men's clothing also was cut out of the cloth woven by their hands and made up, neatly and nicely. Most families had looms and could weave. Warping bars, reels, quilting machines and swifts were used in preparing to make cloth. All this was done by our noble women in addition to helping in the field in busy times – at such tasks as corn planting, harvesting and many other things."

Huffman's childhood recollections of other things will be included in upcoming articles, on and off in the months to come.

Operating an Old "Up-and-Down" Sawmill in the 19th Century (1840s – 1850s)
Article of 9/9/2004

Once again we turn to the incredibly valuable recollections of James Huffman and his experiences as a boy in Page County. Few people understand the process of a modern day sawmill let alone the operations of a nineteenth century sawmill. However, Huffman, in his *Ups and Downs of a Confederate Soldier*, gives some fascinating descriptions. Note that Huffman titled his book for the memory of his days at his father's up and down sawmill and how they also reflected the ups and downs in his life.

Between 1848 and 1850, Huffman was put to work at the mill as a helper. One of his quickest realizations was that if they ever "let the mill stand idle just a few minutes, father would want to know the reason why." Huffman also remembered that the land around his father's property encompassed some of the "best timber in the section of our country."

"On our up-and-down mills we set the front end with an iron crowbar, holding a little wooden gauge against the saw with one hand and moving the log over the bar with the other hand, until it was exactly the gauge, then driving in the sheer to hold it. This went astride of the saw. The other end of the log rested on a slider which was moved with a small handspike, first driving in a needle against the post and moving it until the gauge fitted in. Then we pulled the gate and turned on the water. The rear end was fastened with a wooden key. All this and more had to be done every time. A pin in the carriage beam would thrown the gate when the saw got to the end of the log. This seems to be a very slow process, yet we cut several thousand dollars' worth of lumber each winter. After taking the saw timber off the land, we cut all the sound wood left into cordwood and burned it instead of coal for the furnace which was close by [Huffman is referring to the furnace on Naked Creek], then at a suitable time set the remainder afire. The fire sometimes blazed as high as the trees, cleaning up this land and adding it to the farm, ten to fifteen acres at a time."

Huffman continued later in the chapter . . . "We dared not let the mill stand long, for two reasons. First, the water would overflow;

second, father would overflow. Sometimes he paid us by the hundred for night sawing. One time he promised a nice suit of store clothes – sometimes we had never worn – if we would be industrious and keep the mill going. Well, when the sawing season was over, he went down to Harper's Ferry and settled with the Government, put the money in a shot bag, all gold – from one dollar to twenty dollars denomination – nearly half a bag full. Then one Saturday we went to the store where the tailor met us and took our measurements. He used the finest satin lining that could be had. When my suit was finished and I put it on, I didn't know which way to look or how to walk or what to say. I really think it was the nicest suit I ever wore. Father always gave us what he promised – even to a 'licking.'"

Huffman recalled that in taking the lumber aboard boats bound for Harpers Ferry, he had "considerable experience in boating down the river and made a good many trips." "We could take on one boat from six to ten thousand feet of lumber – according to the tide and weight of the lumber."

More on Huffman's boating lumber down the Shenandoah in another article to come in the future.

Memories of the Apple Harvest in the "Old Days"
(1840s – 1850s)
Article of 10/28/2004

Since we are well into the month of October, truly the time for most apple harvesting is past. However, there are still a few late fall crops of apples to be taken from the trees. Apple butter has been and is still being made and apple cider still runs freely from the presses. But what was it like in the early 19th century in Page County? So far, I've located one good source that gives a glimpse into the old ways and traditions that went along with the apple harvest.

In *Ups and Downs of a Confederate Soldier*, James Huffman recalled that not long after his family arrived at their new home on Naked Creek in the 1850s, they found a "heavy crop of apples." Huffman wrote:

"You know the old-fashioned good mother would not let a bushel of apples go to waste if she could save them. We gathered in the best, to be cut at night and dried, and then washed the inferior apples, and stomped them with malls in a trough, which was dug out of a log, until thoroughly mashed. We then put the mash in a crib upon a platform, under a heavy beam, one end of which was mortised in a tree, the other end worked up and down by a lever and pins as a log-lifter."

"With the crude appliances we made cider for enough kettles of apple butter to last for two years, for fear we would not have apples the next year. Then we made cider for vinegar of all the apples not used for other purposes. One summer we had so many apples we took a load down to a still and got about half a barrel of good brandy, which was used only for medicinal purposes. I think we had that brandy when the war began. I was in the army when the sale was made therefore I do not remember."

"Mother used much strategy to get the apples cut and to keep us awake. She told many stories. If we were very stupid, she told us witch stories. We had a dry kiln, with a flue covered with iron plates and a chimney and could dry apples, rain or shine, nicely and quickly."

Regretfully, that was the extent of Huffman's written recollections. However, it is interesting to see that at the time of Huffman's boyhood experiences, Page County was the leading county in the Shenandoah Valley in value of orchard products. In the first year of recording such things for the census records (1850), Page County was shown as producing $3,769 in orchard products – only Clarke ($3,740) and Frederick ($3,276) coming close in competition at the time. However, over the next ten years, the importance in orchard crops began to decline in Page – the county falling to third in value of orchard products with $9,982 while Rockingham ($16,351) and Augusta ($15,229) took the lead and Frederick coming up as a strong fourth with $7,518.

Five years after the Civil War it appears that a true boom in orchard economy was being realized in the area. However, the decline was continuing in Page. At that time, Augusta County ($52,796), Rockingham ($42,790) and Frederick ($42,033) had taken the lead and Page had fallen into fifth place ($10,133) behind Warren County ($12,507) but still ahead of Shenandoah County ($7,896).

Despite these revealing figures, the 1870 census was the last to record value in orchard products. By 1880, the importance in the agricultural census had shifted to tallying the itemized details in grain (barley, buckwheat, Indian corn, oats, rye and wheat) production.

American Civil War

Cliff Cottage and a Famous Poetess of Luray (1860 – 1865) Article of 10/17/2002

Now used as county office space on Court Street, just opposite the county courthouse, Cliff Cottage was built ca. 1845 by Nicholas W. Yager for his daughter, Mary Overall Yager, on land given by Gabriel Jordan to his son Francis Hubert "Frank" Jordan. Mary was the first wife of Frank Jordan and died in 1849, leaving Frank as a widow with two children. In 1851, Jordan married Cornelia Jane Matthews, the daughter of Edwin Matthews, one time mayor of Lynchburg. Cornelia had received her education at the Academy of Visitation in Georgetown, District of Columbia.

At the time of the war, Jordan had been a lawyer for several years, but preferred to be a teacher, in which occupation he was listed in 1860. The 1860 census listed Frank, Cornelia and the two children from Frank Jordan's first marriage as well as a 17 year-old free mulatto, Elizabeth Syrus. While Jordan went off to serve as his older brother's (Gen. Thomas Jordan) adjutant general, Cornelia gained fame as a Southern "poetess."

In 1863, while visiting her husband in Corinth, Mississippi, Cornelia wrote her poem "Corinth." Due to its "objectionable and incendiary" content, not long after the publication of *Corinth and Other Poems of the War* in 1865, Federal General Alfred H. Terry ordered copies seized and burned in the courthouse yard in Lynchburg. Ironically, a poem that appeared in Cornelia Jordan's first work, *Flowers of Hope and Memory* (Richmond, 1861), included a poem titled "A National Hymn for the New Year," which differed greatly in viewpoint from her later controversial poem "Corinth." Ultimately, it exhibits the belief of many locals who were devout Unionist in 1860, and then later strongly Confederate after the 1860 election of Abraham Lincoln as President and the subsequent call for 75,000 troops. A portion of the 1860 poem follows:

Shall gaunt Disunion hovering nigh
To our bright flag destruction bring,

While, 'mid the brooding shadows dark,
Our Eagle droops his wounded wing?
No! show Thy face, Almighty God,
While peril stalks on every hand;
Stretch forth thine own all-powerful arm,
And save our own, our Native Land.
God of the Year! receive our prayer,
In this our Country's trying hour;
Unveil Thy face--stretch forth Thine arm--
And save us by Thy mighty power.
So shall our praise be of Thy name,
Our glad hosannas all of Thee,
As o'er Columbia still shall wave
The banner of the brave and free.

Other publications of the poetess include *A Christmas Poem for Children* (Lynchburg, 1865); *Richmond: Her Glory and Her Graves* (Richmond, 1867); and *Useful Maxims for a Noble Life* (1884).

Luray Native Started Network of Confederate Women Spies (Summer 1861)
Article of 8/22/2002

Two years ago I wrote an overview about Page County's only Civil War general, Thomas Jordan. Jordan not only served as General P.G.T. Beauregard's adjutant general, but was also a successful author, editor and is still held in high regard today by some Cubans as a heroic figure and, ironically, leader in that little Caribbean country's efforts for independence not long after the American Civil War. It is hard to believe that the pitifully deteriorated old house on Main Street in Luray, once known as the fabulous Mansion Inn and shown in no less than half a dozen postcards from the late 19th and early 20th century, was the house in which Jordan spent a few of his teenage years before launching his very full life, beginning with his matriculation at West Point in 1836.

Nevertheless, with some new research, it appears that yet another achievement can be chalked-up to Jordan's extensive list of life accomplishments; that being the one who began the famous women's spy network in the service of the Confederacy.

Apparently, the night before Jordan joined Beauregard's staff in May 1861, the Luray native dined with future Confederate spy Rose O'Neal Greenhow. Giving her a code and a phony address to his alias (Thomas John Rayford), he asked her to send him military intelligence. From Jordan, Greenhow also learned the use of a 26-symbol cipher, and "began to exploit her connections with the prominent Unionists for the purpose of eliciting information that she then transmitted in code to relevant figures in the Confederacy." Greenhow and Jordan also devised a means by which she could convey significant information to him or to their trusted assistants by raising and lowering the shades of the windows on one side of her house. Over time, Greenhow and Jordan enlisted the regular help of various others, forming an extensive spy ring that included both men and women. Greenhow was later credited with providing Beauregard with vital information that contributed significantly to the victory at First Manassas on July 21, 1861. The day after the battle, Jordan relayed a message to Greenhow stating that "Our President and our General direct me to thank you. We rely upon you for further information. The Confederacy owes you a debt."

A lesser-known spy known to have been recruited by Jordan was Mary "Mollie" Edwards Pultz, of Berkeley County, (then Virginia). The 17-year-old, according to one account, was "very beautiful; tall, fair and queenly in bearing and manner an amiable disposition that ingratiated her with those of all ages and possessing a keen sense of humor." Ultimately, Pultz, like Greenhow, and even Belle Boyd of Warren County, were taken into custody for their activities by the Federal army and held in captivity for short terms in the Old Capitol Prison in Washington, D.C.

Jackson's First Efforts at Burning the Bridges of Page County (April 1862)
Article of 11/22/2001

Nearly a month after the battle of Kernstown, Gen. Thomas J. "Stonewall" Jackson's command was situated near Harrisonburg and was enroute to join Gen. Richard S. Ewell's division in the Elk Run Valley near Conrad's Store (present day Elkton). To better secure this haven for reorganization, on April 19, 1862 Jackson dispatched his mapmaker, Jedediah Hotchkiss, to burn the White House, Columbia and Red Bridges that crossed the South Fork of the Shenandoah River in Page County.

From the outset Hotchkiss' chore was plagued with problems. In addition to a heavy rain, a number of the 150 cavalrymen that Hotchkiss had joined for the assignment at Shenandoah Iron Works were under the influence of "apple-jack." Among these men were Captain George Frederick Sheetz's Hampshire Riflemen of Co. F, 7th Va. Cavalry and Captain Macon Jordan's or Page County's own Massanutten Rangers of Co. D. Jordan had been one of Hotchkiss' students from Mossy Creek Academy in Augusta County.

After finding the men in a foundry, Hotchkiss recorded making "a short halt for refreshments at Mr. Henry Forrer's" shortly thereafter.

As the mission continued ten miles to Red Bridge, Lieutenant Mantaur's squadron (not identified in the roster of the 7th Va. Cavalry) was ordered, along with Hotchkiss' aid, S. Howell Brown, to remove the planking and prepare to set fire to the stringers. Hotchkiss continued on for six miles with Jordan's and Sheetz's companies, likely along the River Road, toward Honeyville, near Columbia Bridge. Sending a scout ahead to reconnoiter, there was no immediate evidence of Federals found at Columbia. Hearing this, and about a mile from the bridge, Hotchkiss allowed the men to feed their horses and "get out of the deluge of rain."

In the meantime, Hotchkiss went ahead and ordered Sheetz and 50 men (another account lists only three men) back to Columbia Bridge to burn it. Additionally, he ordered 1st Lieutenant John Henry Lionberger, of Jordan's company, to proceed with a squadron of sober men from Jordan's company to the White House Bridge near

Luray and destroy that as well.

At Columbia, Sheetz and his men "had put hay in the mouth of it and set it on fire, when a column of the enemy appeared and fired a volley and their dragoons charged." At once, Hotchkiss ordered the men to their horses and told Jordan to front his men. Hotchkiss then went forward to reconnoiter. Instead of attending to his men, Jordan followed. When the Federal cavalry came charging up and firing, Jordan's men "broke at once, except some 3 or 4, and a perfect stampede of them took place, the enemy pursuing for 3 miles, every attempt to rally was unavailing, some actually throwing away their guns, many their coats, blankets &c, &c."

The Federals continued to pursue Hotchkiss and the remaining men for three miles, capturing only a few of the Confederates. Hotchkiss made it to Red Bridge and S. Howell Brown saw to its burning.

Meanwhile, at White House Bridge, Lionberger's squadron met a similar fate. As the Federals pressed the squadron, Private Charles C. Wheat was killed, earning the fate of the first killed in military action in Page County. A boulder, erected sometime after the war, stands on the South side of Rt. 211 (on top of the hill near the Hamburg intersection) to mark the spot of his death. He was buried in the Wheat-Forrer-Kendrick Cemetery in Luray.

Captain S.B. Coyner and Redemption for the Massanutten Rangers, Part 1
(April 1862 – June 1862)
Article of 12/27/2001

Following the botched efforts at destroying the three bridges in Page County on April 19, 1862, "Stonewall" Jackson was again faced with the need to finish the job.

Having successfully driven General Nathaniel Banks' army from the Shenandoah Valley in late May 1862, Jackson's "foot cavalry" had little time to rest in the wake of victories. While one Union army under General John C. Fremont was bearing down from the North, another under General James Shields was pressing toward the Page Valley. If Shields could move quickly enough to overtake Jackson's force in the main Valley, he and Fremont could unite and attack with a numerically superior force. Accordingly, Jackson made a rapid retreat along the Valley Pike toward Harrisonburg. In order to delay Shields advance, the Columbia, White House, and Conrad's Store (Miller's Bridge) bridges needed to be destroyed.

As with April 1862, the Massanutten Rangers of Co. D, 7th Virginia Cavalry were called upon for the task. However, since the April episode, things had changed.

Captain Macon Jordan had since moved on for staff service. In his place, Augusta County native Samuel Brown Coyner had been elected to command. A lawyer and resident of Illinois at the opening of the war, Coyner had returned to the Valley to defend his home in the wake of the John Brown attack on Harpers Ferry. He along with his unit – the West Augusta Guards - were present at the Brown's hanging.

Though he wished to raise a company of his own following the secession of Virginia, Coyner first served as a member of Co. D, 52nd Virginia Infantry, with the understanding that he would be transferred to the cavalry before he was mustered-in. Instead, he was mustered in immediately. However, within a month, Coyner was offered a horse by Macon Jordan in his Page County company. The two being former schoolmates under Jedediah Hotchkiss (by then "Stonewall's" mapmaker), the opportunity was quickly accepted by Coyner. The process was expedited with the aid of Jordan's brother, General Thomas Jordan.

Serving first as a private in the Rangers from August 1861, the 6'1", blue-eyed, 24 year-old quickly earned the respect of his comrades. At Romney in the fall of 1861, Coyner's performance was so impressive as to have been recommended for a captaincy by Macon Jordan.

According to a memoir written by Coyner's brother-in-law and based upon Coyner's letters, diary and other accounts, on the morning of September 25, "Coyner was in the thickest of the fight . . . while charging the enemy who were retreating across the river and attempting to hold the ford and bridge, was in the advance and parried saber cuts with a big, burly Irishman, who evidently had been at Donnybrook Fair, when he saw a head hit at it, but Coyner was too quick for him and almost severed his head from his body, and with a yell kept on in a gallop, 'Hurrah for Coyner!' met his ear, and the gallant command never slackened its speed until they forced the enemy to a hasty retreat. Many were wounded, many killed and many captured; and among the horses captured was this Irishman's horse by Coyner, who up to this time had rode Capt. Macon Jordan's horse called "Tom."

On April 28, 1862, Coyner received the rank and command of the Massanutten Rangers.

Captain S.B. Coyner and Redemption for the Massanutten Rangers, Part 2 (June 1862 – September 1863) Article of 1/3/2002

By June 1862, Captain Samuel Brown Coyner and his Massanutten Rangers were eager to remove the blemish of the April 19 fiasco. Though to no fault of Jedediah Hotchkiss, this time the bridge burning effort was tasked to "Stonewall's" chief of artillery – Stapleton Crutchfield.

Coyner's company moved out toward Page County at 2 p.m. on June 1, 1862. Of the trek, Coyner wrote his sister;

"I must write you a hasty letter and then lay me down to sleep. We have had stirring times since I saw you, and part of those times we, ourselves, were stirred. Never was a General in a worse situation than Jackson on last Saturday and Sunday, and never did a poor being work harder for the preservation of his army than I did."

"Through wind and rain, darkness and sunshine, mud and dust we went, and we conquered. On Sunday, about two o'clock an order came for me to scout in Page, and if necessary burn the two bridges over which it was thought Shields would attempt to cross from Luray to New Market and surround Jackson. We set out on aforesaid march and about eleven o'clock that night received further orders to burn the bridges immediately."

"We were then at Mount Jackson, at least fifteen miles yet to travel and nearly all the horses broken down. We pushed on and about half way up the mountain were overtaken by one of the most dreadful thunder-storms I ever experienced. We were compelled to wait in the erode until it stopped raining and cleared off before we could move on, and then half the time moved only by the flashes of lightening. About half way down the mountain the storm was repeated. The rain fell in torrents, and the thunder rolled. And oh! the darkness was so thick I could almost catch it in my grasp. But still we struggled on, and my men clung to me like children to a parent. The safety of Jackson's army and perhaps of our country demanded it, and though they suffered; they seemed to suffer willingly. We reached the bridges and they were in flames by sunup."

"That evening (Monday) the Yankees pitched their tents and planted their cannon by the smoking ruins. We remained in Page that day and night, and the next morning orders came to burn the Conrad's Store bridge if necessary. We started, but oh! the roughest road! For two miles at one place we had to almost crawl. We arrived at five o'clock, the enemy had been there--and left about one half hour. Soon the bridge was on fire and then Providence intervened; the windows of Heaven opened, the floods came and Jackson was safe."

Coyner continued to lead the Page men of the Massanutten Rangers from the Valley and beyond Gettysburg. During the entire time, Coyner found time for a love of his own amongst the women of Page County. Known only as "Miss Dovel," it seems likely that she was the sister of one of Coyner's horsemen.

Out of all of the company, the Dovel family provided more men for the Massanutten Rangers than any family in the Page Valley. But who had the sister that stole the captain's heart? Perhaps a Dovel family member knows today.

As to how severely she broke the captain's heart remains for the next article.

Captain S.B. Coyner and Redemption for the Massanutten Rangers, Part 3
(September 1863)
Article of 1/17/2002

Simply known as "Miss Dovel," by September 1863, Coyner was left broken-hearted. Again, in a letter written from camp at Brandy Station to his sister at Mt. Solon, he wrote on September 4, 1863:

"Love stories and live gossip are out of the question, especially for one who has learned the "stern realities" of life in war and peace; and moreover, for one who wins sweethearts and loses them on small and false pretenses as I do. You have heard of my last misfortune haven't you? That sweetheart of mine of such longstanding, Miss Dovel, has deserted me—has deserted her Captain in the hour of trial. She has left the ranks of my little Spartan Band, and gone over to the enemy. I report her on my muster rolls--Deserted August 2nd, 1863--Let her go--Poor thing! Little does she know what a glorious cause she has proved unfaithful to, what a garden spot flowing with milk and honey she has exchanged for a land of barrenness (?) and wild growth. Matrimony, though state of wretchedness and love, thou land of shackling railroads and broken telegraphs, muddy pikes and unfenced fields, snarling cats and barking dogs! I may emigrate to the wide plains some day."

On September 13, camp life was interrupted when the Rangers were once involved in a fight with Federal cavalry near Culpeper Court House.

After over an hour of combat, the 7th Virginia had been driven back to the edge of a woods. Under a terrible artillery fire of enemy grapeshot, Colonel Thomas Marshall attempted to rally his regiment, but failed. According to the history of the unit, Marshall turned next to Coyner to rally his men alone and was successful.

What followed next was written as conveyed in stories to Coyner's brother-in-law:

"Capt. Coyner was leading about twenty-five remaining of his gallant company as the regiment started back. Capt. Coyner called to his men, 'Come on boys, follow me!' His company was headed towards Mountain Run. On meeting Gen. Custer, who had come on the field with the balance of the Second Brigade, our little band was about to be driven back again, when Capt. Coyner called to his men 'Steady--close in on the center--Forward!' when Lieut. George W. Summers, Capt. Coyner's second Lieutenant, heard while riding with his captain the fatal 'thud' and Capt. Coyner remarked, 'George, they've got me this time,' and turned his horse and either Sergeant Long or Private Kite, and Private Davis caught their gallant Captain as he was about to fall--the blood gushing from his left leg. Just then the bugle call sounded for a retreat. They led Capt. Coyner's horse as far back as the Gruinon house, through the woods, when they halted and bound up his wound and then carried or conveyed him to Orange C. H."

Once in Orange, Coyner was taken to an old hotel. Cousin Will Coyner of Co. F saw to it that his family was notified at once. On September 15, sister "Maggie" and her husband set out and arrived at 8 p.m. By 11 p.m., the gallant leader of the Rangers was no more.

Later buried at Mossy Creek Church Cemetery in Augusta County, a fellow soldier wrote of him: "As a soldier he possessed all the attributes that make a hero."

June '62 Cavalry Clash at Luray
(June 1862)
Article of 8/8/2002

Ever wonder if there was more to that gray sign on Rt. 340 North, near the Ruffner House in Luray? The Department of Historic Resources signs are great, but are limited to so many words to describe a person or incident. Though the Union cavalry probe of June 1862 was not a major incident, it does warrant some additional detail.

Weeks following the battle of Port Republic and within days of the departure of Shields' Federal troops for Front Royal, Federal cavalry patrols were deployed to the Page Valley to find the disposition of Jackson's troops, whom the Federals believed might still be in the area.

On June 22nd, a detachment of the 1st Michigan Cavalry approached Luray and took reports from "the Negroes that general Ewell was in Luray in force and that Jackson had sent to Richmond for reinforcements." Federal Maj. Charles H. Town noted, "Union people reported the enemy in force in and about Luray. By June 29, following a "sharp skirmish" with Confederate cavalry at Milford on June 24, Col. Charles H. Tompkins, leading a cavalry contingent consisting of companies from the 1st Vermont, 1st Maine, and 1st Michigan set out from Front Royal toward Luray.

Late in the day, the contingent had probed as far as present-day Compton before returning to Milford. Saddling the horses by 4 a.m. the following morning, the Federals continued their advance upon Luray.

The first action opened between 8 and 9 a.m., within five miles of Luray, near Big Spring, as Corp. Barney Decker of Company D, 1st Vermont Cavalry, captured a Confederate cavalry vedette. As the small force moved on, two companies of Confederate cavalry, consisting of about two-hundred men, were encountered, here near Yager's Mill, on "the hill about half a mile out of Luray . . . in a line just outside of the town upon the New Market or Gordonsville road." As the Federals moved in for the challenge, one company from the 1st Maine and another of the 1st Vermont moved in support. As the columns of horsemen assembled, a charge was made, successfully dispersing the Confederates who lost two men captured. From the ranks of the Federals fell one man from Co. D, killed, and one of the 1st Maine wounded.

Maj. Angelo Paldi of the 1st Michigan Cavalry continued the advance through Luray, and was ordered by Col. Thompkins to overtake the Federal cavalry that was still in pursuit of the Confederates. Moving out along the New Market to Sperryville Turnpike, at least four miles, Paldi halted and "perceived that our cavalry must have diverged from the road, as nothing but scattered rebels could be seen, and they far ahead." By 9 p.m. the Federal force that had reconnoitered to Luray was back in camp near Front Royal.

Page County Civil War Christmas Past:
In the Field and at Home
(December 1864)
Article of 1/1/2003

At present, the known resources for Christmas experiences of Page County soldiers in the field during the Civil War are few and far between. The first of any diaries, letters or memoirs known to touch on, at least the date of December 25, is that of James Robert Modesitt. However, writing to his wife from Port Royal in Caroline County on Christmas Eve, Modesitt makes no mention of the holiday. The diaries of John P. Louderback ("Riverton Invincibles" of Co. I, 10th Va. Inf.) and Capt. Michael Shuler (commanding the "Page Grays" of Co. H, 33rd Va. Inf.) either skip the event altogether because of furloughs or simply because the diaries end beforehand.

To come even remotely close to the experiences of what Page County men may have experienced during Christmas 140 years ago, one, for now, has to refer to other resources. One member of one of the other Valley companies (from other than Page) of the 10th Virginia Infantry recalled simply "Everyone seems to be BLUE. If ever I had the Blues have them now. Most lonesome day I have spent since in the service."

Interestingly, Christmas recollections of Page County soldiers during the Civil War that do exist are those of soldiers being at home recuperating from wounds in 1864. Lt. George Daniel Buswell, of Co. H, 33rd Va. Infantry, was one such soldier. Ironically, in the wake of the horrible "Burning" of October 1864, one would think things rather grim in the county. However, Buswell painted quite the different picture. As early as Thursday, December 22, 1864, the lieutenant wrote of sleighing to school and that the "boys turned the teacher out at noon." A few days later, on Sunday, December 25, Buswell spoke of Christmas and of drinking eggnog and then on to a family members house where there was a "nice crowd present." In the days that followed, dancing seemed to be the business of the day through New Year's Eve. On December 26, Buswell, in a crowd of folks, and along with Lt. Oliver Hazard Perry Kite (also of the Page Grays and also recovering from a wound), headed for Mr. John Welfley's where "they had a dance." The following day there was another dance at Jack Kite's. With a brief respite from the dance on December 28, the pleasant pastime resumed once again with yet another dance at Noah Kite's (Alma), followed by yet another on New Year's Eve, at Mr. Leonard S. Printz's house.

While merriment may have not be so readily available in the field, the opportunity for dancing amidst the company of fine friends and "lady-folk" was certainly a welcome fare for a soldier home on furlough or convalescing from, what some soldiers refer to as that "million dollar wound."

Encounters in History: Union Soldiers and their Accounts of Page County Slaves Article of 2/27/2003

As resources are regretfully few and far between describing firsthand the experiences of both free blacks and slaves in the early history of Page County, a handful of accounts are out there to allow a small peak into that aspect of history at the time of the American Civil War. To date I have been fortunate to locate at least three personal recollections of Union soldiers passing through the county in 1862 and 1864. While they are only minor contributions of a history of social interactions, they do contribute a great deal considering the void of information previously available on the subject in the county, especially at that particular time. Sometimes, those who give the accounts might even offer an interesting sidebar just because who they were.

Regretfully, though he left no record of meeting slaves in Page County, a significant character in black history entered Page County in early May 1862. Enroute to reinforce Union forces at Columbia Bridge then threatened by Gen. R.S. Ewell's Confederates near Somerville Heights, the 2nd Massachusetts Infantry arrived in Page on May 6 and bivouacked for two nights near "Berner's Mills" before recrossing the Massanutten to New Market. With the Bay State men was 25 year-old 1st Lieutenant Robert Gould Shaw who, less than a year later, was commissioned colonel of the 54th Massachusetts Infantry, the first regiment of black troops in the Union Army.

But, as for the accounts . . . though two accounts given for May 1862 by members of the 39th Illinois Infantry and the 4th Ohio Infantry gave fantastic insight into the social interaction between the Union soldiers and slaves near White House Bridge and at Hamburg respectively, one from 1864 gave much more. Union Colonel Charles Russell Lowell, Jr., commanding a Federal brigade that was in the midst of pushing Confederates from Luray, gave what may be the first, and perhaps only known written account that clearly documents a Page County slave leaving with the Union army. Having been involved in the action at Yager's Mill on September 24, Lowell paused briefly a few days later in Staunton to write his wife of his time in Page County. "I haven't told you that, the day before yesterday in Luray, I organized a small black boy, bright enough and well brought up; his name is James, but as we have already two of that name about here, I call him Luray, which is quite aristocratic. You can teach him to read and to write this winter, if you have time. The Doctor thinks you would find more satisfaction in him than in your pupils of Vienna."

It is interesting to note that Lowell's wife, Josephine, was a sister of the aforementioned Col. Robert G. Shaw. Though Col. Lowell was later killed, Josephine was quite active for the balance of her life in significant charitable projects. Regretfully, little is known (yet) as to what happened to the young man that Col. Lowell renamed for the town in which he was found.

Stories from the Old Soldiers:
"Around the Camp Fire of Co. K"
(ca. 1863)
Article of 8/5/2004

In February 1914, the *Page Valley Record*, a local newspaper with a short life span, ran a series of articles about some of the activities of the men from Co. K, 10th Virginia Infantry – the "Page Volunteers." These stories, given to the newspaper from the veterans directly, gave a rare and sometimes comical view of soldier life that was otherwise filled with a great deal of suffering.

One story centered around two men of the company and the "Battle of Fairfax Station" that ensued between the two men.

"This engagement took place between John B[orst], our Quartermaster Sergeant and Private Philip R[oberts?], both of Company K, was all over a pint of flour which the Quartermaster claimed he issued, and which the Private was equally positive that he didn't. The battle raged furiously, the tide turning first one way and then the other, until the boys interfered and stopped the fray. The attitude of the private soldier to the officer immediately over him was different in the Confederate Army from that of any other army in the world. The private obeyed orders from his officers, but when his private rights were invaded, he was as quick to call the officer's attention to it as if he was a brother private. This independence of spirit in the private was a valuable trait, especially in the hear of battle, when officers were stricken down and confusion might ensue therefrom except for a presence of mind and ability of a number of privates in most of the Confederate company to immediately take command and direct the movements of the company as his officers would."

Another story was a humorous one but showed the determination of the Page County Confederate . . .

"We were expecting a battle, but didn't know how soon it would be. Regiments were changing positions and there was a general stir within our lines whose meaning was very clear even to the private soldier. The sentinels and pickets were posted for the night. Philip's [Philip M. Printz] was at the end of a road which wound in and out of our lines. He was instructed by his Sergeant of the Guard that in case more than one man came his way to let them advance one at a time and give the countersign. Along towards midnight, Philip's alert ears detected a large body of troops in motion. The tramp, tramp of many feet became more and more distinct., and it was evident that they were approaching his picket post. It was not long before a Colonel at the head of his regiment was in hailing distance, Philip called out in a clear, steady voice, 'Halt! Who goes there?' The answer came back, 'Colonel ____ of the ___ Georgia and his regiment.' Philip came back, 'Advance Colonel ___ of the ___ Georgia and his regiment, one at a time and give the countersign.' The Colonel answered, 'My God man! That would take all night to pass my regiment, I have one thousand men with me.' Philip repeated his command, 'Advance Colonel ___ of the ___ Georgia and his regiment, one at a time, and give the countersign.' 'Call the Sergeant of your guard,' snapped the Colonel, and his one thousand men growled at the delay. The Sergeant of the guard came, and Philip remonstrated with him that he was obeying orders and that the regiment couldn't pass unless they 'advance one at a time and give the countersign.' The Sergeant of the guard rushed off, woke up the Captain and brought him hurriedly to the scene. The Captain passed the Colonel and his regiment upon the Colonel's countersign alone."

"The old soldier who related this incident of Philip's soldiering said of Philip: - 'He was one of the best men in the company. There was no better soldier in the whole army of Northern Virginia and I don't think I'm putting it too strong to say that his superior could not be found in either army of our civil war. He would obey orders to the letter if he knew positively that in doing so he would be killed in the next minute."

The Tale of a Humorous Civil War Era County Prank, Part 1 (ca. 1862) Article of 11/28/2002

There is no doubt that many a good ol' country boy prank is played from time to time amongst friends. Interestingly, one such prank from some 140 years ago was well documented in the October 1894 issue of *Confederate Veteran Magazine*. Well, uh, it was a prank, but it wasn't necessarily the "boys" that were the major players . . . But to the subject of the story . . .

An 18 year-old farm boy and native of St. Joseph, Tensas Parish, Louisiana at the opening of the Civil War, Benjamin Drake Guice originally enlisted with Company D, 6th Louisiana Infantry on June 4, 1861 at Camp Moore, Louisiana. By September 1862, Guice was on the sick call list and sometime after that, had parted company his Louisiana comrades. On January 13, 1863, Guice enlisted in Co. D, 7th Virginia Cavalry ("Massanutten Rangers") in Luray.

In a letter dated August 10, 1894, Guice recalled a humorous tale of being in Page County with some Page County comrades:

"I went one night in company with a comrade to call on some young ladies, and as the country at that time was infested with the boys in blue, we agreed to stand guard alternately while the other fellow went in and chatted the young ladies, and I noticed, too, that my comrade was very willing for me to take the first turn in the house, although he acknowledged he was as hungry as a wolf. I was very much in love with one of the young ladies of the house, and I thought that she reciprocated. When I walked into the house my best girl met me at the door and took me into the parlor. I asked the question, 'Where are your sisters?' She said they had gone to a neighbor's to stay all night. I was pleased with that, for, as my comrade's best girl was gone, he would not object to standing guard all the time.

'Now, Ben,' said my lady love, 'I have been looking for you to drop in to night, and I have ready the nicest supper I could prepare; so just give me those cumbersome pistols that you may eat with some pleasure.'

I had left my saber in the saddle. 'No, I thank you Miss Nannie. I cannot part with my pistols: there are too many yanks around here.' But her bright eyes and lovely smiles disarmed me. She just wanted 'to have the honor of holding them' while I ate my supper, but she slipped my pistols in a sideboard drawer and turned the key on them.

The Tale of a Humorous Civil War Era County Prank, Part 2 (ca. 1862) Article of 12/12/2002

While we last left Guice thinking he was about to consume a sumptuous feast, his recollections of the event, in fact, would have initially spoiled a meal for any number of hungry Confederates. "As I finished a good supper two blue coats opened a door on one side of me, and two entered by another door behind me, and all four of them leveled their pistols at me and commanded me to surrender. To make the matter more real, my girl threw herself on her knees at my feet, put up her hands to the Yankees, and begged piteously for them not to shoot me, and one of the bluecoats said, 'Well, Miss, for your sake we will not shoot him, but you must be responsible for his good behavior while we eat our supper.' Then one of them said: 'Your arms, sir, quick!'

Having explained that he was already disarmed, Guice continued. "One of them leveled a pistol at me and said: 'No fooling now, Johnny; give up your arms.' And then Miss Nannie said: 'O Mr. Yankee, please do not shoot him! I will get his arms for you.' And off to the sideboard she flew to get my arms. During this stage performance my comrade stood on the outside on the gallery looking through the window. I saw that he was shaking his sides with laughter, and in a second it occurred to me that I was not being taken prisoner by real Yankees; so I made a break for him, running over the Yankees; but he knew what was coming, and jumped off the gallery, and hid. By the time I got back to the dining room the Yankees had disappeared, and my best girl met me with a smile and said: 'Forgive me, Ben; the girls forced me into this.' I told her she had better take to the stage, for it was the best 'forced' performance I had ever witnessed. The Yankees were her sisters and a young lady neighbor, who had dressed themselves up in Yankee uniforms and laid a trap to capture me. I very coolly told my best girl that she could have made the capture without any assistance whatsoever.

There is but one of those girls living to-day, and my comrade too has crossed over the river, but many persons yet living in Page Valley remember it well, for it was many a long day before I heard the last of it. The boys used to try to tease me about the matter. I would turn them away with the remark that I would not give a cent for a soldier who would not surrender to four pretty girls."

On a sadder note, barely a year before writing the recollection of the incident, Guice had submitted a query to the same magazine requesting to hear from another former comrade from the Page County company. Isaac A. "Ike" Gaines, was, however, like Guice, from a Louisiana Infantry regiment, perhaps even Guice's old company, and had enlisted with Guice in Luray. "In September 1865, on my way to my home in Tensas Parish, La., from the Army of Northern Virginia, I parted on the wharf at Memphis, Tenn., from my old comrade, Ike Gaines . . . and since then have never heard a word from him. I have written letters of inquiry to several newspapers, but to no effect, and now write this to you with the hopes that some one will see it that knows or knew him, and tell me of his whereabouts or of his fate. It would afford me much pleasure to hear from him, as we went through many hard struggles and trials together."

A detailed postwar roster by Page County Confederate veterans stated that Gaines may have had the surname "Gainous" and had, in fact, served with a Louisiana Infantry regiment prior to his time with the Page County unit. Sadly, the same source of information on Gainous also revealed the possible reason why Guice had not been able to reach his old comrade. Apparently, after his release from the wharf at Memphis, Gainous "on [his] way home was killed by Yankees."

A postwar resident of Natchez and Woodville, Mississippi, there is no indication that Guice ever learned the fate of his old comrade. A member of Camp No. 20, United Confederate Veterans in Woodville, Mississippi, Guice died on October 6, 1922 in Natchez, Mississippi and was buried in the Natchez Cemetery.

James Jewell "Exchanges Himself" from Captivity
Part 1
(1864 – 1865)
Article of 10/14/2004

James W. Jewell was born ca. 1845, the son of Augustus and Nancy "Fannie" Jewell. A resident of Hope Mills at the opening of the Civil War, James, at around the age of 17 years of age, joined Co. K, 10th Virginia Infantry (the Page Volunteers) on March 17, 1862. Jewell seems to have faired well in the army for sometime and did not see any large personal difficulties in health (or at the mercy of a Union minie ball) until May 12, 1864, when he was among the many captured in the attack on the Confederate earthworks at Spotsylvania Court House. However, even then, "Jim" Jewell wasn't quite the type to give up just yet.

From a letter written in 1914 from Dr. Theodore H. Lauck (formerly of the Page Volunteers) to Summers-Koontz Camp Commander Frederick T. Amiss, Lauck conveyed the story of just what Jewell did to remedy his status among those in captivity.

After having been marched off from Spotsylvania, the Confederate POWs were taken to Belle Plains Landing on Aquia Creek before they ended up at the POW Camp at Point Lookout, Maryland a few days later. According to Lauck, they had only been at the Point but a few days before he missed Jim Jewell at the roll call.

Lauck continued; "Now for his history, as told by himself at Little Washington, thirty-nine years afterwards. He had told me in 1901 of some of his experiences, and so at my next meeting with him I asked him how he managed to procure an exchange, when none of us left behind could accomplish it. "Why, I exchanged myself," said he, to my great astonishment and then he explained his Yankee trick that certainly beat the band a big Yankee band at that." While in the Union POW Camp, Jewell had told Union Maj. Bradley that he "wanted to take the oath, and having taken it, agreed to enlist in their army, but not seeming too eager to do so." Jewell continued that "The Division I belonged to was soon sent to the coast of North Carolina and I soon had the pleasure of being put on outside picket duty. When night came on, good and dark, I stole away from my post and struck out North West towards where I knew Dixey Land lay, and next day reached Goldsboro, and lounged around the depot, waiting for a train to Richmond. Citizens noticing my blue uniform, began to crowd about me and looked like they wanted an explanation, if not an apology. I was enjoying the situation fine, and waited until one of the crowd asked me where I belonged. I told him that I belonged to the 3rd Va., Inf. Brigade. Then someone cried out '3rd Va. Brigade? Why we have a Regt. in that Brigade, that was enlisted in this city.' 'Which one', asked Jim. 'The 3rd' was answered. 'Well, said Jim. I went over the breastworks at Spotsylvania C.H. soon after I did on the 12th of May, being gobbled up by the Yankees.' They asked him why he was in blue clothes. He explained, and then one of the party told him that the Col. of the 3rd had a home and a wife in the city, and that she had never received a line from him since the 12th of May, and did not know whether he was dead or alive. They almost forced him to go to the home of the Colonel and relieve the mind of his wife all that he could."

James Jewell "Exchanges Himself" from Captivity, Part 2 (1864 – 1865) Article of 10/21/2004

Having taken "liberty" of prisoner of war camp by volunteering to "don the blue," sometime between June and September 1864, Jim Jewell had left his Yankee "comrades" for a return trip to Virginia and his friends and comrades of Co. K, 10th Virginia Infantry. While at Goldsboro, North Carolina, Jewell gave a small degree of comfort to a concerned wife who had not heard from her husband since Spotsylvania Court House. According to his account, all that he could tell was the story of the capture, and that he did not think that there was any loss of life her husband's regiment. She was greatly comforted by the interview, and fed him well, and made him exchange his hated uniform for a suit of citizens clothes once worn by her husband.

Theodore Lauck recalled of Jewell's story that the wife filled Jewell's haversack, and "I think, supplied him with expense money, for his run to Richmond. At the latter city he boarded the first train to Staunton, he could catch, without getting a pass from the provost and that mistake led him into a hitch in his plans when he got to Staunton. A small sized homeguard youth arrested him on the platform as a deserter or as absent without leave because he had to confess that he had no pass. He spent the night under guard, and in the early morning asked the little soldier to please go with him to a spring on the out skirts of town. He noticed as he walked along beside the guard that there was no percussion cap on the musket the boy carried, so when he had bathed his face and filled his canteen, he remarked 'your gun is not loaded.' 'Oh, yes it is, but we are not allowed to have any caps,' replied the unsuspicious raw one, in close contact, with an old one, for the first time in his service. Jim gave a short laugh, and heading towards home said, 'Good morning, my son, and walking away rapidly, left the boy gasping.'"

Lauck continued of Jewell's story, "He reached Harrisonburg before the night and was delighted to run right on to Col. [D.H. Lee] Martz, who had by some rare good fortune, got exchanged just two weeks before. He asked the Col. where the rest of the boys were and when he expected to return to the army. The Col. told him he would leave as soon as his furlough was out, and expected to find the army of Gen. Early near Strasburg. Jim told him that he would continue on home to see his folks and get a change of underclothes, and would return to duty in a week or so and here the eyes of the gay narrator widened and sparkled with amusement."

Jewell stated, "Sonnie, I got to Fishers Hill the very night before that devil of a stampede." Lauck continued tat "The upshot of that experience was that the crows and buzzards saw a very tired Jim sneaking across the near-by river and Fort Mountain, and scurrying across two Valleys, to reach the humble cabin above Kimball he had left just two days before."

"While he rested and got the soreness out of his legs, he did some bushwhacking 'on the side,' and along with Clarence Broaddus shot at two chicken-stealing Yankees. Jim missing, and Clarence knocking his target off his horse, and stampeding the other fellow who dropped his bunch of chickens." Lauck concluded that Jewell later "rejoined the regiment at Petersburg in the winter, and was in every skirmish and battle up to the finish."

Interestingly, Jewell, like Lauck, was initially at the Point Lookout, Maryland POW Camp and then transferred to the Elmira, New York POW Camp. However, military records do not mesh well with the accounts given in the story. While Lauck stated that he recalled the day when Jewell was missing in roll call while at Point Lookout, Jewell was transferred to Elmira in July 1864 and, a month later, Lauck was transferred to Elmira. Certainly Lauck and Jewell would have certainly grouped up together with the rest of the Page Countians at Elmira. On top of that, military records reveal that Lauck was released from Elmira on June 19, 1865 and Jewell was released over a week later from Elmira on June 27, 1865 giving us a little genealogical research lesson in an otherwise great story – that the military service records we research may not always be accurate.

Where were the Confederate Soldiers During the Burning? (October 1864) Article of 9/11/2003

When the Union soldiers under Col. William H. Powell came to call upon the barns and mills of Page County in October 1864, there was little to no resistance standing in the way of the burnings that followed. So, where were the Confederate troops? As the "Burning" was in the wake of the terrible defeat of Gen. Jubal Early's Confederate forces at the Battle of Fisher's Hill, the Confederates in the Valley were in no shape to stand in the way of Gen. Philip Sheridan's devastation of the Valley from Augusta County on down to Page. However, as many local men in the ranks of the Confederate army were with Jubal Early just to the south of (and constantly on the heels of) Sheridan's forces, "battles of opportunity" were available to those who were permitted to take leave of the army and engage isolated elements of Sheridan's men in partisan fashion.

It has been quite sometime ago but I've touched upon the subject a few times with the articles on the affair at the Hershberger House as well as the articles on the execution of the two Marylanders in response to the "bushwhackings." However, a letter written to the *Page Courier* in March 1891 by Benjamin Drake Guice (the subject of another earlier article) gives insight into yet another encounter during October 1864. Reflecting warmly upon his time with his comrades from Page County, Guice, a Louisianan by birth, had eventually come to serve with the men of the Massanutten Rangers after his discharge from the 6th Louisiana Infantry.

A part of Guice's account follows:

Who was it that went with me to save uncle Reuben Lucas' barn from the torch of two Yankees, half drunk, and telling the girls if they would kiss them they would not apply the torch to the house and barn, as they had been ordered to do. If I mistake not it was old Reuben Walton. I can see ourselves now as we galloped down the long lane to uncle "Rube's" home, well knowing that if they discovered us before we reached the barn yard that they had a dozen chances to kill us, where we had one to kill them. As we galloped in I told "Rube" to take the man tat the barn and I would look after the one at the house. Imagine my surprise when I rode up to the fence between myself and my Yankee and presented my pistol and called out "surrender," when the young lady jumped between Mr. Yankee and myself and screamed out "Don't kill him Ben; they will burn us out sure then," and at that very instant Mr. Yankee leveled his carbine at me over her head! Sad plight, think you, but with lightening speed I dropped from my horse, and through a crack in the fence and before he knew where I had gone had my pistol under his nose and my left hand grabbing his carbine. I had hardly accomplished this before I heard old "Rube" exclaim, "Mount, you cuss! I have no time to parlaver here with you," and in less than had the time it has taken me to write it we were galloping back down the long lane, with the Yankees between us, and as we rode back Mr. Yankee hands me his canteen with the remark, "Boss, have some "bounce," and I accepted his invitation to drink, and in drinking recognized, the good old cherry bounce" of my old friend John Shuler, of which I had often drank before. The Yankee had robbed him of it."

The conclusion and the search for the secret of "Cherry Bounce" to follow.

A Cavalryman's Story and the Secret of a "Family Recipe" (October 1864) Article of 9/18/2003)

After Ben Guice's one-on-one encounter with the Yankee, as Guice recalled, the story had a great deal of excitement left on that day during the Burning of October 1864.

"On that same day I rode up to uncle "Jim" Kite's residence and the family all ran out to meet me and hear the news of the Yankee raid, and I had just threw my foot over little Nellie's neck to rest and talk, when uncle "Jim" exclaimed, 'Dast, Ben, the Yankees will get you this time, and almost at the same instant half a dozen bullets went buzzing by my ears (you know what that buzzing means, don't you boys. It is sweet music, if a fellow does not care what he says). Like a flash, I darted thro uncle Jim's yard, leaped his back fence, and before the Yankees knew the direction I had taken I was across the River, perched in a hill, watching them set fire to uncle "Jim's" barn, and in twenty minutes from the time the Yankees left the barn, I was helping Uncle Jim pull his wagon, wheat fan, and other tools from the burning barn, and when I left him he had all his boys and dogs killing rates, and his parting salute was, "Dast, Ben, we will get rid of the rates, at any rate."

Ben Guice's story goes on and gives some great insight into a few scenes where his comrades of the old "Massanutten Rangers" were involved in a few scrapes. One thing of great interest however that was of particular interest was that, though he was not a native of Page County, he always felt at home with the families of his comrades. "Never shall I forget that time [February 1865] you were at home with your loved ones around you, and I far from home and friends, but truly can say that I was at home in every house I entered, the pet and spoiled boy of you all, but your parents also."

As an interesting turn in the story, in reading the portion of the letter about his "old friend" John Shuler's Cherry Bounce, I realized that Guice had apparently made a warm acquaintance with one of my ancestors; John Shuler, in fact, being my great-great-great grandfather. As that was interesting enough in itself, I really wanted to know about the secret behind the "Cherry Bounce." After asking both family and friends in Page, nobody seemed to know the answer behind the family recipe. So, when most else fails in research, I turned to the Internet and searched for the secret and, alas, it really isn't much of a secret at all. In fact, Cherry Bounce goes back at least to American Colonial times as a very popular social drink, made of one's favorite liquor (usually rum, bourbon, brandy or corn liquor), a lot of cherries and, of course, sugar or honey. While the basic idea behind the drink was revealed, regretfully, one secret does remain . . . that being the actual contents of John Shuler's personal recipe.

One Page County Confederate and John Wilkes Booth (June 1863) Article of 11/14/2002

Now, some reading the title of this article are going to think I'm right off the rocker with a lot of the other wild stories that have surfaced in Page County over the years. However, this one is for real. I think it would be more entertaining to give this in a Paul Harvey "Rest of the Story" method, but this is in print, so you can technically cheat and look at the end.

Actually, this one Page County Confederate did not necessarily have anything to do with Booth directly, but rather in an indirect fashion.

During a fight on June 24, 1863, several of Mosby's Rangers, including the noted Page County Confederate (a captain at the time), got in a tight scrap with some Federals of the 16th New York Cavalry. According to an article published in the *St. Louis Post-Dispatch* in 1895, after the Rangers had captured a good number of the "Yankees," one particular trooper continued to give the Rangers a fit from behind a persimmon tree and in a ditch with a seven-shooter repeating rifle. Three attempts were made to capture this Federal trooper before success was finally had.

Once the trooper had been overtaken, one of the junior officers leapt from his saddle, clearly enraged for having to make three attempts to snatch the foe, knocked the Spencer rifle from the Yank and pointed his pistol at the fellow's head. The Page man yelled out: "Don't shoot that man! He has a right to defend himself to the last!" The weapon was lowered and the Federal trooper was hauled off to Richmond as a prisoner of war. Had the Page County officer not called the junior officer off, surely the Yank would have met his demise.

Eventually taken to Andersonville, the Federal trooper was luckily released prior to Union Gen. U.S. Grant putting an end to the exchange of prisoners. As fate would have it, following the assassination of President Abraham Lincoln, the trooper was among 26 others that surrounded a barn at the Garrett Farm in Port Royal, Virginia. That trooper, none other than Sergeant Thomas P.

"Boston" Corbett, won fame for having shot Booth, Lincoln's assassin, through a crack in the barn. Corbett was initially arrested for disobeying orders, but was later released and awarded his share ($1,653.85) of the reward money. Known as a "religious fanatic," Corbett later explained his actions saying that "God Almighty directed me."

The Page County man was, of course, William Henry Chapman, later John S. Mosby's right hand and second in command of the famous Rangers.

It is interesting to read more about Corbett's life, his peculiar pre-war activities and his being institutionalized for insanity in later years. After his escape in 1888 from the Topeka Asylum for the Insane, Corbett was never heard from again.

Isn't it often interesting to examine events and how the slightest alterations in history might have changed something a few years or several years down the road?

The Final Resting Place for Federal Dead in Page County (1866)
Article of 7/25/2002

There are a few books on the history of Page County that discuss how Federal agents arrived in the county after the war and removed Union soldiers to a National Cemetery. Established in 1866, Staunton National Cemetery is the final resting place for at least 232 known and 521 unknown Federal soldiers buried between Lexington and Luray and some points into West Virginia. While it is unclear as to how many unknown Federal soldiers were relocated from Luray and Page County, the following five soldiers taken from the county are positively identified: 1) Plot 97: Pvt. Arthur Collinson (Callison); 2) Plot 170: Sergeant J.W. Putney, 5th New York Cavalry; 3) Plot 270: William G. Kilby, Co. C, 2nd New York Cavalry; 4) Plot 235: Jesse Maris, Co. C, 6th Ohio Cavalry; 5) Plot D 281: William Robinson, 13th Indiana Infantry.

Interestingly, only Maris has confirmed service with the unit designated on his headstone. Born September 4, 1840 in Salem, Columbiana County, Ohio, Maris appears to have died during the Federal occupation of Luray during the summer of 1862. Kilby is also recorded as having died at the same time (July 1862), but his name is actually not listed in the New York compiled records, so he may have served from a different state.

Though his unit is not identified on his headstone, records reveal that Collinson (Callison) was a member of Co. F, 6th Ohio Cavalry. He was one of two men killed in that unit and buried in October 1864 at the Hershberger Farm near Luray. Though he is likely buried in Staunton, curiously, Callison also has a headstone in the Grafton National Cemetery in Grafton, West Virginia. Callison was a native of Clark County, Ohio and had enlisted on February 11, 1864. By the time of his death, he had yet to receive his full enlistment bounty.

The second man buried at the Hershberger place was likely carried away and buried at Staunton as an unknown soldier. However, once original documentation of the disinterment is examined and cross-referenced with the records of the 6th Ohio, the unknown stands an excellent chance at identification.

As another twist in identification, William Robinson, listed as having been a member of the 13th Indiana Infantry and having been originally buried at the Jackson Shuler Farm, is an error altogether. William Robbinson (note the spelling difference) was a member of Co. E, 13th Indiana Infantry and, by October 1862 was discharged for service in the 4th United States Artillery. Though the man buried in plot D 281 in Staunton was likely a member of the 13th Indiana and either a victim of disease or even a casualty of the Somerville Heights fight on May 7, 1862, it certainly is not Robbinson.

Putney is also a mystery, as he is not listed in the master index of Union soldiers from the State of New York.

Details from Page's Southern Loyalists Claims, Part 1
Article of 12/11/2003

In an article from December 1998, I covered the topic of the Southern Loyalists Claims records for Page County. It was just an overview at that time, but, as a detailed examination this year proved, there is much more to the documents than initially meets the eye. To review briefly, the loyalist claims had allowed Southerners who had been loyal to the Union to file claims against the United States government for provisions/items requisitioned and/or taken as a result of the war. The Southern Claims Commission, in Washington, D.C., handled these claims and remained flexible in that it extended the deadline for application several times before finally closing acceptance in March 1880. Out of Page County there were 45 applicants, of which only 5 claims were actually allowed and paid. This article will focus on those claims that were either disallowed or barred from reimbursement. Regretfully, of the 40 applications disallowed or barred, only fifteen remain on file at the National Archives in Washington, D.C. Whatever happened to the remaining barred/disallowed applications is a mystery.

Interestingly, as I had also pointed out in the article from 1998, some of the applicants had actually served as Confederate soldiers. Additionally, as the applications proved, some of the claimants, though they had given supplies to Union soldiers, had also sold supplies or equipment to Confederate forces. On the other hand, some had sons who fought for the Confederacy . . . but did that make one disloyal? In the end, there is a lot of speculation that can circulate around the stories behind these applications, but where is the concrete truth? Were some filing the applications in good faith and with complete honesty; were some ill-informed as to the specific criteria of the application process; and/or were some simply exaggerating the truth in order to secure government money when they were in severe need of the money? Remember that this "glimpse into the past" is purely speculative as it is hard to prove, without further documentation and after over 140 years after the fact and without the applicant in front of you to give further details.

To support these claims, affidavits were taken from those who knew the claimant and his background during the war. However, the

Federal government was not simply satisfied with the affidavit of a local who might have also been friends with the applicant and who was just trying to help the claimant to secure Federal money. If the slightest suspicion of disloyalty surfaced in the review process, a government investigator was put on the case and oft-times found, albeit minor in most cases, that there was evidence that may have questioned absolute loyalty. Ultimately, it didn't take much for an investigator to charge the applicant as a disloyal individual, no matter how small the "infraction," as will be seen.

Fourteen of the fifteen applications remaining on file at the National Archives are revealing to varying degrees; those of Samuel A. Buracker, Isaac Cullers, Martin Hite, J.W. Kibler, Joseph Miller, Albert Pressgraves, John H. Pressgraves, Morgan M. Price, Emanuel Snyder, John Sours, William H. Sours, George Summers, Samuel Varner, George Viands.

An overview of details of thirteen of these applications will follow in the next article.

Details from Page's Southern Loyalists Papers, Part 2
Article of 12/18/2003

Of the remaining existing applications for Southern Loyalists Claims from Page County, a few reveal just enough information to show why they were disallowed. While they had provided Union forces with supplies and/or forage, Samuel A. Buracker, John H. Pressgraves, Emanuel Snyder and John Sours were probably all disallowed because they had also sold goods to Confederate forces . . . once.

Other applications get into a bit more detail that tied into the individual vote in the public referendum (May 1861) in support of Virginia's secession. A few of these men were also militiamen, which in no way defined a certain fact that they were loyal to the Confederate cause, but coupled with the vote for secession, probably put their cases further into the improbabilities of being approved.

Joseph Miller simply noted that he was obliged to vote for secession through "fear."

Martin Hite noted that he had been "persuaded to vote for the adoption of the ordinance" but he also had served as a member of Co. I, 97th Virginia Militia, had been called into service and was tasked with guarding Union prisoners at Libby Prison in Richmond for three months.

According to Morgan M. Price (a member of Companies K & F of the 97th Va. Militia), at the time of the public referendum vote, he felt that it was not safe to go to the polls and vote against secession. "The only man who voted against secession had to leave immediately to save himself from the mob." When Federal troops occupied Luray in July 1862, Price was taken to Front Royal by Federal troops where he insisted on taking the oath of allegiance and was released. After Gen. Franz Sigel's men left Luray, some were left behind sick or were stragglers. Taking these men into his home and feeding them, Price claimed that he also "piloted them through the mountains" and out of what had become Confederate lines once again. Nevertheless, his application was still disallowed.

William H. Sours had, according to his claim, been loyal and at the beginning of the war. "My sympathies were with the Union Cause. I did not talk much in favor of the Union. I had to be careful how I expressed my sentiment. I feared that I would be arrested if I spoke much."

J.W. Kibler, once a sergeant in Co. M, 97th Virginia Militia, despite having given articles to Federal troops was refused payment, at least in part, because he on August 20, 1862 had signed a petition circulated in the county to have Dr. William H. Miller released from the Camp Chase, Ohio POW camp so he could "fulfill his duties as their physician."

Samuel Varner had voted for secession because, as he claimed, he was told if he "wanted peace he must vote for secesh."

George Viands had a claim that was disallowed rather easily as it was well known that he had been directly involved in the production of iron during the war at Speedwell Forge.

In addition to this information, a few of these men revealed that they had sons in the Confederate service but also stated that they had not supported them during the war. At the forefront of such claims stood that of George Summers. In the next article, Summers' application will be reviewed and will prove quite revealing. As many know, Summers was a Union sympathizer in an extreme way, yet he lost much during the war, including his only son.

The Revealing Southern Loyalist Claim of George Summers, Part 1
Article of 1/1/2004

The most revealing of all fifteen remaining barred and disallowed Southern Loyalist Claims from Page County was that of George Summers of Grove Hill. For starters, Summers was well-known to have been an extremely loyal sympathizer to the Union throughout the war, and, in the end, was totally broken-hearted for what he received at the hands of Federal forces at the end of the war . . . his only son (Confederate Captain George W. Summers) executed without trial. While certainly the act of the execution of his only son was bad enough, the deception by Federal soldiers to a well-known Union sympathizer was a real betrayal of the faith that Summers had held in the cause that he had believed in, despite the punishing repercussions that came to him for it throughout the war.

Nevertheless, Summers' story was a very well documented one for the record. His application was extremely detailed as were the affidavits supporting the application.

According to his application, Summers mentioned his only son's service for the Confederacy but clearly stated that he was "bitterly opposed to it." He had proposed that his son "go North to go to school there" and had even purchased him a horse to take him out of the area that would become the endangered arena of war. However, when the war came, the younger Summers went off to war on the horse that his father had purchased for him. In time, his son sent back the horse for having secured another upon which to ride in the engagements to come. The elder Summers reaffirmed that he had, in fact, furnished his son with "anything as I did when [he was] at home" but did not believe that to qualify him as a Southern sympathizer.

Feeling that Confederate money would not hold its value, Summers mentioned in his application that, at the opening of the war or just before, that he had partnered with William H. Forrer in the purchase of tobacco in Maryland. Summers wrote, "I invested in tobacco and had a one-third interest in 2,000 pounds of tobacco which was taken to Maryland." Summers and Forrer, apparently, made several trips to Berlin, Maryland during the war, and on one such trip, in early

1863, the partners were arrested and taken to Baltimore. Brought before Union General Robert C. Schenk, the men explained their situation and, with the assistance of a local attorney (Daniel Miller of the firm of Daniel Miller and Co.) and a heavy bond (which appeared to read, if my eyes did not deceive me, a whopping one million dollars!), the men were released. Schenk also issued the two permits to cross lines as necessary to secure supplies for their families and others with Union sympathies. Likewise, and apparently in the same trip, the tobacco was turned over to the men and sold "for greenbacks and bankable Maryland money."

Upon returning to Page, Summers and Forrer were threatened with arrest by Confederate authorities but the threats never materialized. "A party of soldiers were sent to me," noted Summers, "but were preventing by the fullness of the river from marching my home. The Confederate Cutthroats took my goods, burnt my rails - - - - upon me as they pleased."

While this particular run-in with Federal authorities did not take place until 1863, the year before had actually proved to be the first run-in. More on that story in the next issue.

The Revealing Southern Loyalist Claim of George Summers, Part 2
Article of 1/8/2004

While George Summers appears to have had troubles at the hands of both Confederates and Union soldiers throughout the war, apparently they began when the opposing forces arrived in Page County in April 1862.

As Union troops moved into and occupied the area, Summers had received protection orders for his mercantile stores from Col. John P. Hatch of the US Army. However, and as was typical, after Hatch went on ahead with his command, Union troops who followed up behind had little regard for such orders. In May 1862, as Gen. James Shields' army passed along the River Road toward Grove Hill and eventually Port Republic. Despite his loyalty to the Union, Summers' store became subject to pillage. Wrote Summers, "A portion of his army camped near my store three or four days. Living on the other side of the river from my store and not anticipating any damages from Shields' Army encamped close by, I went to my house at night as usual. Shields' army passed during my absence and carried off my whole stock of goods and merchandise, which amounted to around one and two thousand dollars when I got to my store in the morning. The house was broken open and everything gone. My papers were strewn along the road towards Port Republic for several miles. I had a general apartment as is usually kept in a country store, Boots, shoes, hats."

As Summers struggled to maintain proof of his loyalty to passing Union commands, he also placed himself in a bad position in what was Confederate territory. John Welfley recalled, because of Summers' outspokenness regarding his loyalties, he had "Heard a great many parties threaten him with arrest saying that --- as he ought to be killed that such men as he caused a great deal of trouble in the army." Samuel Step had made a similar statement in another affidavit and had "heard men say Summers ought to be hung that he be to stay her I was alarmed for him." Summers himself recollected that, during the time of Ewell's camping in the area in April 1862, a Major Wheat (probably Rob Wheat of the Louisiana Tigers) and Capt White "told me that if I uttered one word more" regarding his

Union sympathies, "a thousand men would kill me." Yet he remained "unmolested at times I felt that my life was at stake."

Summers again fell victim to the Federal army during the Burning of October 1864 when Col. Powell's cavalry took three horses from Summers' property. After gaining an audience with Powell personally, Summers was given permission to search the camps and have his horses returned. However, Summers not "knowing the full extent of the camp and having no guide I found only two." A 6 year-old Sorrel could not be located and as Summers later stated, he never "received pay for him."

While Summers upheld his claims of loyalty through the claims application process, the claims commission investigator discovered that Summers did aid the Confederacy on at least two occasions. Whether the aid was made under duress or was voluntarily is another question. In December 1861, Summers sold as much as five bushels of wheat and hired out six 4-horse wagons and teams for 17 days at $5 per day and another eight 2-horse wagons and three 4-horse wagons and teams to the Confederate Army of the Kanawha. In all this amounted to a profit of $1,072.00. But did he get the wagons and teams back? He also was found to have sold 3,500 pounds of hay and 39 ½ bushels of wheat to passing Confederates (likely cavalry) in March 1863.

Postwar Pensions for Page County Confederate Veterans, Part 1
Article of 3/11/2004

In the years following the Civil War, there was a great movement in the way of veteran care. While the U.S. Government had provided pensions for veterans of earlier wars, there was little more in the way of compensation (other than bounty/land grants). In the case of the Civil War veteran, organizations such as the United Confederate Veterans and Grand Army of the Republic (Union) both made great strides for improved veteran care. While the GAR had the backing of the Federal Government and a strong lobbyist group, Confederate Veterans, obviously, could not rely on equal support from the Federal government and turned to the governments of the respective states that had been a part of the Confederacy.

In turn, there were huge efforts made by the respective states. As early as 1867, the Virginia General Assembly enacted legislation (ending in 1894) to provide artificial limbs and other disability benefits to Virginia's Confederate veterans. To coordinate the program, and oversee the distribution of aid, the Assembly established the Board of Commissioners on Artificial Limbs. As a part of the process, injured soldiers submitted certificates from their county court stating that they were Virginia citizens, that they had lost a limb or had been otherwise disabled in the war, and what assistance they required. The veterans also listed the command in which they served; included information on when, where, and how they were wounded; and provided details about their medical history.

These records are on file at the Library of Virginia in Richmond, and, according to their website, "These disability applications provide a strong sense of the Civil War's impact on individuals, families, and communities. In truth, many veterans found the postwar battle for economic survival and physical mobility nearly as difficult as the war itself."

In all, fifteen Page County Confederates applied for this program including Samuel E. Bailey (Co. D, 7th Va. Cav.), Benjamin Franklin Beahm (Co. H, 33rd Va. Inf.), William Larkin Dulaney (Co. D, 7th Va. Cav.), Isaac C. Jenkins (Co. L, 10th Va. Inf.), John Wesley

McCoy (Co. H, 33rd Va. Inf.), James Harvey Mayes (Co. D, 7th Va. Cav., Paul Miller (Co. H, 33rd Va. Inf.), Gideon S. Printz (Co. K, 97th Va. Militia), James Thomas Purdham (Co. H, 33rd Va. Inf.), Jacob Shenk (Co. H, 33rd Va. Inf.), Peter Sours (Co. H, 33rd Va. Inf.), Joseph F. Stover (Co. H, 33rd Va. Inf.), Tillman Shumate Weaver (Co. K, 10th Va. Inf.), William S. Yates (Co. H, 33rd Va. Inf.), and Martin L. Young (Co. K, 10th Va. Inf.).

For more information and to see these applications online, refer to the following websites:

For Page County Confederate disability pensions:

http://ajax.lva.lib.va.us/F/NFSGR39BIB43Q9LUV221E6572124IF2
MKS8HNTHNUVYUEN-08238?func=find-
b&request=page+county&find
code=WSU&adjacent=N&x=55&y=11

Postwar Pensions for Page County Confederate Veterans, Part 2
Article of 3/18/2004

By 1888, the Virginia General Assembly had taken additional steps in the way of Confederate Veteran pensions and passed pension acts in 1888, 1900, and 1902, and a series of supplementary acts between 1903 and 1934. The act of 1888 provided pensions to Confederate soldiers, sailors, and marines disabled in action and to the widows of those killed in action. Subsequent acts broadened the coverage to include all veterans, their widows and their unmarried or widowed daughters. The acts required that applicants be residents of Virginia. Later legislation included veterans or their survivors residing in the District of Columbia as well.

All applications contain statements pertaining to the service record of the applicants and may include medical evaluations, information about the income and property of the veterans or their widows, and, in the case of widows, the date and place of marriages. The collection also includes claims submitted by more than five hundred African-Americans who had worked as cooks, herdsmen, laborers, servants, or teamsters in the Confederate army.

Nearly 350 Page County Confederate Veterans and/or widows applied under this program. A review board, composed partly of local Confederate Veterans (former Rosser-Gibbons Camp Commander John W. Grove was the Secretary of the Page Co. Pension Board from 1902 through the 1920s), reviewed each application and decided on the award amounts according to several different factors. Those who were awarded monthly stipends were veterans who were either partially disabled ($15 per month) or totally disabled ($30 per month). However, the disabilities might not necessarily be as a result of war and were often postwar ailments that were common for the aging at that time. Though the criteria was not specified on how one could qualify for the maximum allowable under the pension guidelines, there was at least one Page County Confederate who received $50 each month. Qualifying widows were usually awarded $25 a month compensation.

Not all persons who applied for pensions were rewarded a monthly allowance. For starters, applicants who had taken the oath of allegiance to leave prisoner of war camps prior to the close of the war were among those disapproved. However, those who had served in the militia received particularly critical review. Though the 97th Virginia Militia had been called into the field on and off for nearly nine months from 1861 – 1862, few former militiamen were approved for pensions. The militiamen had been disbanded in the spring of 1862 and were offered the chance to join a regular field unit or, often, were later conscripted if they met the age qualifications that continued to expand as the war went on. If a militiaman did not show initiative to join a regular field unit though he was of age and physical condition to have done so, such submitted applications were dropped without hesitation.

Widows also met the same level of scrutiny in their applications. If their husbands served in the militia, the applications were not approved. Furthermore, if a veteran's widow had remarried since the death of her veteran husband or the widow did not marry a veteran until after May 1, 1865, pension applications were denied. At a later point, the pension boards later eased the rules to include widows who had married veterans in years after the war.

For more information and to see these applications online, refer to the following websites:

For Page County Confederate Pension rolls (after 1888):
http://ajax.lva.lib.va.us/F/YCLYVPJJ8LV4IB7TTNBLJ5H5YUNUC3VHF7289Q4TEDHCCS1X33-06348?func=find-b&request=page+county&find_code=WSU&adjacent=N

Page County Confederates and the R.E. Lee Camp Soldiers Home Article of 3/25/2004

Accepting applications as early as 1884, the Robert E. Lee Camp Soldiers Home in Richmond, Virginia served to "Prevent honorable and brave Confederate soldiers, who by wounds and disease contracted in the service of their country, and not in their old age are unable to support themselves, from dying in the county almshouses." The Robert E. Lee Camp of Confederate Veterans was initially the spearhead behind the project and the home was bought and paid for and equipped by the R.E. Lee Camp, No. 1, Confederate Veterans. For two years it was supported by their private funds. In 1892, the home entered into contract with the Commonwealth of Virginia, by which $30,000 a year was received for a period of twenty-two years, at the expiration of that time, the Home would become the property of the Commonwealth of Virginia. Originally, the $30,000 in support money was intended to support 200 veterans. However, the Home increased to over 250 veterans by the late 1890s. As costs escalated, there was an increased appeal to the Commonwealth for additional support. In eight years, the State appropriated $173,805 while the Lee Camp raised $149,563 nearly matching the state funds.

While the history of the home is much more extensive than can be explained in this article, the Soldiers' Home continued to operate through 1939 and took the applications of at least seven residents of Page County. Of the seven applicants, three were never admitted. Of the three - Jacob S. Snyder, a member of Co. H, 33rd Va. Infantry applied in 1908 from Gordonsville but was rejected from admission because he had deserted during the war; James W. Short, a member of the Rosser-Gibbons Camp, was approved for admission in 1917 but lost the paperwork and, though he reapplied in 1918, died in early 1919 and missed another opportunity for admission; Rosser-Gibbons Camp member and former Co. D, 7th Va. Cav. private Thaddeus W. Mayes applied in November 1935, but, by the time he was approved later that year, he was extremely ill, dying on January 18, 1936 as one of the last three Confederate Veterans in Page County. Comrade Charles Robert Hilliard died two days later on January 20.

Of the four men admitted, Sutton J.H. Will, formerly a member of the Dixie Artillery, suffered from paralysis and entered the Home on Feb 2, 1903. He died on June 25, 1905 and was buried in Hollywood Cemetery, Richmond. Abraham Booton Shenk, formerly of Co. D, 7th Va. Cav. and another Rosser-Gibbons Camp member had applied and been receiving a pension since 1903. However, his condition worsened and was admitted to the Home on January 22, 1917. He died on January 6, 1920 and was brought back to Page County and laid to rest in the Hamilton Griffith Cemetery. Though not a native of Page County, Thomas Griffith Read, Co. I, 33rd, applied from Page County and was admitted on January 21, 1893. He died on January 3, 1895 and was buried in Hollywood Cemetery. Lastly, John Henry Lentz, formerly of Natural Bridge, Rockbridge County, moved to Page County in the late 1880s and settled near Verbena. A former member of Co E 1st Battalion Virginia Infantry, Lentz had been born in Germany and was working as a gardener in Verbena at the time of his application. He was admitted to the Lee Home on March 16, 1892 and died on January 3, 1902. He was buried in Mt. Calvary Cemetery in Richmond.

Applications can be viewed at:

http://ajax.lva.lib.va.us/F/5AMHAED7S1PE6SCU21REIL1MAUJ5RG3LXCQRQHR3ANU3NBEV86-04985?func=find-b&request=page+county&find_code=WSU&adjacent=N&x=32&y=3

A Brief History of the Two Confederate Veterans Groups in Page County, Part 1 Article of 4/22/2004

There were two Grand Camp Confederate Veterans of Virginia formed in Page County – the George W. Summers Camp # 68 and the Rosser-Gibbons Camp #89. The George W. Summers Camp No. 68 formed in Shenandoah, Virginia and was chartered in 1896 with Commander Robert S. Pritchett and Adjutant James E. Price. Apparently the camp was quick to start the first Sons organization in Page County. The Sons camp was actually called the Page Valley Camp No. 9 of the Grand Camp Sons of Confederate Veterans of Virginia, though in the United Sons of Confederate Veterans (USCV), this was Camp No. 20.

In 1897 the G.W. Summers Camp paid for what appears to have been approximately 44 members. Command also shifted in that same year to Commander Gilbert T. Israel (who was also ran a professional photography studio in Shenandoah) and Adjutant Thomas A. Miller. The camp also sent two delegates to the convention that year – Cdr. Israel and David W. Wyant.

Apparently, 1907 was the last year that the G.W. Summers Camp ever paid dues though they remained on the books of the Grand Camps organization through 1909. It was in 1909 that the overall organization shows the camp as finally disbanded. Nothing more can be found on the Sons Camp beyond mention of it in 1896 and the July 1898 issue of *Confederate Veteran* Magazine. Incidentally, the Page Valley Camp, at that time in 1898, included Commander E.L. Keyser and Adjutant R.H. Cline. Like the Grand Camp, the Sons may have disbanded by 1907 or before.

Though there was an assemblage of Page County Confederate Veterans for the 1881 reunion with Union Veterans, in Luray, the first official organization of Confederate Veterans did not take place until April 30, 1898 with a meeting at the Luray Courthouse. The Rosser-Gibbons Camp No. 89, Grand Camp of Confederate Veterans of Virginia camp charter dues were paid in September of the same year. Then again, on May 24, 1904, the camp was chartered again but this time with the United Confederate Veterans as Camp No. 1561, thereafter-holding dual memberships with both the Grand Camps and the U.C.V.

Information pertaining to the Rosser-Gibbons Camp officers is as follows:

Commanders:
1) Richard S. Parks 1898 - 1913 (died 27 Mar 1922)
2) John W. Grove 1914 - 1915 (died Aug 1924)
3) Charles E. Biedler 1916 - 1925 (died 11/8/1926)
4) ??? 1926 - 1928

Adjutants:
1) William E. Grayson 1898 - 1902 (later Commander of the William Richardson Camp, Front Royal)
2) Silas K. Wright 1903 - 1913(died 12/1/1925)
3) James W. Wood 1914 - 1920 (died 1928)
4) Philip M. Printz 1921 - 1925 (died 23 Oct 1928)
5) ??? 1926 - 1928

A Brief History of the Two Confederate Veterans Groups in Page County, Part 2 Article of 4/29/2004

Apparently, the Rosser-Gibbons Camp was only moderately active in the overall Confederate Veterans organization outside camp activities. In all, the camp only sent delegates to seven conventions of the Grand Camp of Confederate Veterans of Virginia including:

1898 - S.N. Judd (Lt. Cdr in 1898) & John W. Grove (see above)
1905 - R.S. Parks (see above), Middleton W. Yates (died 3/1/1922), T.B. Amiss (died 11/9/1913)
1906 - T.B. Amiss, J.W. Walter (died 7/12/1910)
1908 - M.W. Yates, L.R. Badger? (probably L.R. Bailey)
1910 - J.W. Grove & John D. Printz
1914 - J.W. Grove
1915 - C.E. Biedler & M.W. Yates

Though a definitive list is not available, members of the camp also attended United Confederate Veterans Conventions as far away as New Orleans. Additionally, some Page Confederate Veterans were present at the 50th Anniversary Reunion of Gettysburg in 1913.

Capt. Richard S. Parks was perhaps the most active of all of the members and had extensive service with the Grand Camps Confederate Veterans of Virginia serving as one of four aide-de-camps for 1904, and as a member of the Committee on Legislation and the Committee on Pension Fraud for several years.

Membership in the Rosser-Gibbons Camp fluctuated and is not clearly known. However, based on the annual payment of dues to the state organization, the membership level was as follow (the camp was originally formed in 1898 with 89 members):

1899 - approx. 55 members
1905 - approx. 83 members
1906 - approx. 58 members
1907 - 1914: approx. 70 members
1915 - approx. 87 members
1918 - approx. 87 members

1920 - approx. 87 members
1921 - 1922: approx. 83 members
1923 - approx. 50 members

Fortunately, an obituary written by Philip M. Kauffman on the death of Rev. Harrison Monroe Strickler, gave the facts behind the disbanding of the Rosser-Gibbons Camp. Serving as chaplain for the camp, Strickler (formerly the 1st Lt. of Co. E, 35th Bttn. Va. Cav.) was present at a May 5, 1928 meeting of the camp. The obituary states that on that day, "with only three members present, the camp was disbanded." Following Strickler's death, only two members of the Rosser-Gibbons Camp remained, one being P.M. Kauffman, the same man who witnessed Jackson's crossing at White House Bridge in 1862 and the same who later belonged to Keyser's Boy Company and then later belonged to Co. E, 35th Bttn. Va. Cav. and was almost executed by Union Col. Powell's men during the Burning in October 1864. According to the same 1928 obituary, Kauffman stated that the Rosser-Gibbons Camp had lost three members that year (J.W. Wood, John W. Rothgeb, P.M. Printz) and two the year before (Andrew J. Huffman, Peter Broy).

By the middle 1930s, there was less than half a dozen Confederate Veterans left in Page County. After the deaths of Thaddeus Wellington Mayes (1/18/1936) and Charles Robert Hilliard (1/20/1936), Peter James Keyser, Jr. held the title as last surviving Page County Confederate Veteran, dying almost exactly three years later on January 4, 1939.

The 1918 Confederate Veterans' Monument
Article of 9/5/2002

Throughout the North and South, it isn't uncommon to see a single monument gracing the town square or county courthouse lawn honoring Civil War veterans from the respective counties. However, Luray is among a rather atypical crowd, especially in rural centers, in that it has two Confederate monuments. Ultimately, Herbert Barbee's decision to place his Confederate Monument on the east side of town in 1898 had much to do with him being a native of Page County and that the inspiration itself came from a scene that he had witnessed very near his home in nearby Thornton Gap.

However, by 1912 members of the Rosser-Gibbons Camp #1561, United Confederate Veterans (also known as the Rosser-Gibbons Camp #89, Grand Camp of Confederate Veterans) felt that they had yet to make a true tribute of and to their own. Luray resident, and the first commander of the Summers-Koontz Camp #490, Frederick Taylor Amiss once wrote about the second Confederate Monument in Luray and stated that, prior to 1912, Lieutenant J.B. Seibert "was the originator and moving spirit" in the project. "Mr. Seibert's enthusiasm caused the Rosser-Gibbons Camp of Confederate Veterans . . . to take up the matter and it appointed a Monument Committee, with Mr. Seibert as Chairman" and F.T. Amiss as Secretary and Treasurer, "and selected from the Veteran Camp, the Luray Chapter of Daughters and the Sons Camp others to make up the Committee."

While an initial inspiration in the project, Seibert died in the fall of 1912. As a replacement chairman, former Mosby Ranger, Albert W. McKim (the same A.W. McKim that owned the drugstore) was appointed. The monument was completed in November 1917 by the McNeil Marble Company of Marietta, Georgia, and dedicated on July 20, 1918 (on the 57th anniversary of the First Battle of Manassas and 20 years to the date, after the dedication of the Barbee Confederate Monument).

Though the intent was also to have an ornamental cast iron fence placed around the monument as well as plaques listing all of the county's loyal Confederates installed on the sides of the monument, funds were short, especially in the midst of World War I. Nevertheless, having committed to the project since 1913, F.T. Amiss continued to go to great lengths in talking with and writing to Page County Confederate Veterans in order to collect an accurate listing of the county's loyal Confederates. Ultimately, in compiling the names, he was also greatly concerned about offending descendants by leaving out certain names due to the criteria. In a letter to four chief former officers and non-commissioned officers of the Page Volunteers, Amiss wrote, "We can never build our Monument unless perfect harmony prevails, and I do not entertain for a moment the idea of dictating to any one as to who is and who is not a loyal Confederate Soldier . . .

The Last of Page County's Confederate REAL SONS
Article of 4/24/2003

So often do historians hope to find some real tie, one last link to the respective periods of history that we find most fascinating. Books are great, letters are better, but real people can sometimes be the very best.

While some may find it hard to believe, there actually is at least one remaining REAL SON of a Page County Confederate Veteran! Retiree Albert Lee Comer of Western Maryland was born in 1921 as the last son of then 74 year old Confederate Veteran James John Comer.

Born May 2, 1847, James John Comer was a son (one of at least eight children) of John and Delilah Kite Comer. Shortly after the outbreak of the Civil War, while the family was residing near Comertown, James was one of the first to volunteer with Company H, 33rd Virginia Infantry (the "Page Grays") on June 1, 1861 at the extremely young age of 14. The youngest member of the 33rd Virginia Infantry and, perhaps the entire Stonewall Brigade," James was quick to feel the sting of battle and was wounded on July 21, 1861 at the First Battle of Manassas. Returning to duty by August 11, 1861, James' only left ranks without permission once, from March 21 to April 1, 1862, to check on his family. While only a few pages of his diary still exist, in March 1863 James wrote sentiments that were upon the minds of many soldiers from both North and South during that winter; "it is hard times & I fear wors[e] is coming the best hope for peace is gon[e] this day closes with trouble upon [sic] my mind this World is a wilder-ness of wo[e]." James' record continues to show exemplary service for the balance of the war, being wounded once again at Chancellorsville on May 3, 1863 and then captured on July 20, 1864 and sent as a prisoner of war to Elmira, New York. He was one of the few fortunate enough to be exchanged (on March 4, 1865) before that practice came to an end. Just short of the ripe old age of 18 at war's end, James had seen more than what many would see in a lifetime. However, for the time, he was one of many from his generation to be "touched by fire."

In 1869 James married Mary Ann Strole. After eight children and by 1904, James was a widower. However, and in the spirit of a documented number of prolific Page County Confederate veterans, in 1907 James married again, at the age of 60 to 27 year old Lucy D. Sly. Lucy would outlive James, but would also bear at least seven more children. Albert Lee Comer was the fifteenth and last child. Nine years later, the Confederate Veteran, whom Albert knew better as, as one newspaper put it in 1999, "the blacksmith and farmer" who "pulled the Shenandoah Valley family through the tough years of the Depression" died and was buried in the UMC Cemetery in Shenandoah.

After a visit to Gettysburg in the summer of 1999 and after a bit of research, Albert's niece, Nancy Lantz of Ridgeley, West Virginia, helped make possible the 1999 induction of Albert as a member of the Colonel William Norris Camp No. 1398, Sons of Confederate Veterans in Darnestown, Md. When asked what he thought about being made a member he stated, "I just never gave it any thought really. When I would tell people, they thought I was pulling their leg."

World War I

Following Page County's War Veterans
Article of 5/8/2003

A few years ago I was amazed at a government organization when they said that they finally wanted to begin documenting the history of America's WW1 veterans. As fewer and fewer of the actual veterans from that war are around, why did the idea suddenly become important when it was almost too late to tap the remaining few? Why not 50 years ago? It sounds all too much as if somebody finally said, "wow, we better do something soon because there aren't that many left to talk to anymore" and viola! . . .the right people made things happen and finally there was a program in place to make it happen. In some sense it reflects an ongoing historical dilemma. Ultimately, we live history from day to day, but too often it never becomes REALLY important until the window of opportunity for the best possible information has passed us by . . . usually many years after the actual historic event.

I guess this all comes about as a result of my recently fingering through a copy of *Service Record: World War II, Luray and Community* originally compiled by the Comer-Jones Post 621 VFW of Luray, I couldn't help but wonder about the possibility of expanding upon that work and making the history of Page County's war veterans an actual detailed project. Additionally, while the book was created to focus on Luray's WW2 vets, I also noted that veterans from the rest of the county; including the service records of my grandfather and even an uncle who was captured and served in WW2, were not included. Not an oversight of the project by any means, just data that needs to be collected and included in a supplement or revision.

But then the challenge grows even more. What about an expanded work . . . one which would include the service of all veterans, in their own words? There is nothing more compelling and stirring than reading the actual words of a veteran and his or her experiences in a life that not everyone would have the opportunity, or sometimes even want the opportunity to endure.

That being said, I would strongly like to encourage folks from throughout the county to start looking for those lost letters . . . the ones that the veterans actually sent from the front, whether it be a few days ago, 30 years ago, 60 years ago or more . . . from Manassas and Gettysburg to the Marne; from Normandy and the Pacific to DaNang, Kuwait and even to Baghdad. If those letters exist, aren't they worthy of being documented for posterity sake for generations to come? When you find them, please let me know, and, if possible, send photocopies to begin the compilation of letters, memoirs and diaries.

In the meantime, stay tuned next time for a review of Page's WWI questionnaires. While the numbers of Page County WWI vets was not huge, the stories that some of Page's Doughboys told in the questionnaires are priceless.

Page County's World War I Questionnaires, Part 1
Article of 5/22/2003

Before I begin examining the particular questionnaires that were filled-out by Page's WW1 veterans, I need to give a little history of how the questionnaires came to be.

The Virginia War History Commission was established in 1919 to collect, assemble, edit and publish information and material concerning Virginia's participation in World War I.
From 1917 to 1928, the Commission gathered and published seven volumes of source material, including lists of Virginians honored for distinguished service and guides to newspaper clippings and wartime diaries and letters. It also prepared preliminary manuscripts for a narrative history of Virginia's role in the war. This history was never published. In June of 1928, all of the Commission's records were turned over to the Library of Virginia.

The Commission also conducted a survey of World War I veterans in Virginia through the use of a printed questionnaire. Currently, the Library of Virginia has these World War I History Commission Questionnaires online as a fully searchable database of over 14,900 records, one for each questionnaire respondent, accessible by name, city/county, and race. Each record is also linked to digitized images of each page of the questionnaires, as well as any accompanying material such as photographs and additional pages submitted by the respondents. Page County's questionnaires can be found at http: //eagle.vsla.edu/cg-bin/ww1.gateway?authoity=0006-69580&conf=-10000++++++++++++++

Each questionnaire has four pages:

The first page records information about personal background, including the full name of the soldier; date and place of birth; name of mother and father (and their places of birth); race; religious affiliation; names of wife and children; fraternal orders and college fraternities; education; occupation prior to entering the service; name of employer; residence before and after time in service; present home address.

The second and third pages record details of the veteran's war record, including date of induction, rank, military branch and ID number; military company, regiment and division; where trained or stationed before going to Europe; port of embarkation and debarkation; experiences in action; citations for and details of distinguished services; details of any injuries; discharge; occupation after the war.

The fourth page contains several questions designed to elicit information about how the war affected the serviceman and how he perceived his experiences during the war. The questions deal with the effect of disabilities upon occupation and employment; the serviceman's attitude toward military service; the mental and physical effects of United States camp experiences and of overseas experiences; how the experience affected his religious beliefs; the effect of all of these experiences as contrasted with his state of mind before the war.

In some cases, for the Page County soldiers (incidentally, only 47 filed the questionnaires which equates to around 15 – 18 % of the total number of Page's WW1 veterans) some soldiers submitted a photograph with the questionnaire, often in uniform, signed and dated. Questionnaires with photographs are indicated in the database by a keyword-searchable note.

Page County's World War I Questionnaires, Part 2
Article of 6/5/2003

While there are, at current estimation, approximately 300 men from Page County who served in World War I, only 47 filled-out the questionnaire designed by the Virginia War History Commission. Of the 47 men, only 23 recorded actual combat service. Over half of the number who did not make it to action in France were members of the Student Training Corps at colleges such as VMI (Frederick Thomas Amiss), Roanoke College (Connor B. Batman, Paul B. Broyles, George F. Cook, Jr.) and Muhlenberg College (Albert B. Sherman); members who were discharged due to health or other reasons before embarking for Europe (Raymond F. Campbell, Lloyd H. Level, Ralph O. Rothgeb); members who were drafted so late in the war, and though they may have made it to France, they missed the fighting (Ralph C. Broyles, Ernest R. Clem, Roy T. Sanders, Jessie E. Seal, Ben H. Seekford); those who made it to Europe but were in support roles (Noah F. Painter, Charles Richardson); or those in the Air Corps (Albert M. Chapman). Colonel Robert F. Leedy (a famous Luray resident who deserves an article of his own) was actually one member who originally belonged to the 116th Infantry, 29th Division but ended up as colonel of a camp (4th Pioneer Regt) in South Carolina. For whatever reason (possibly his age and health), he was not permitted to go to France for which he claimed that he would "regret to the day of my death."

The majority of the combatants were either of the 29th (Blue-Gray) Division (Clyde F. Batman, John R. Deavers, Arthur A. Grove, Charles T. Holtzman, Carl A. Kibler, John R. Leedy, Carson G. Mason, Wharton A. Nichols, Charles R. Rothgeb, Carl F. Sanders, John V. Sours, George W. Vogt) or the 318th Infantry Regiment, 80th (Blue Ridge) Division (Leo C. Bradley, Lester Kibler, Samuel D. Price, John M. Sours, Hubert M. Strickler, William M. Turner, Walter I. Brubaker). There were a number of members who filled out questionnaires who served in other units such as the 26th Division (James E. Nicholson/Nichols), 32nd Division (Herbert G. Campbell), 37th Division (Rolandus Aleshire), or in other units undesignated in the questionnaire (Clarence W. Gochenour, W.W. Goldsmith, Elmer Griffith, Fred Purdham, John D. Smith, Marshall

B. Wood). Likewise, there were at least two regular Army officers (Edward M. Almond and Lawrence Young).

The 80th Division was organized at Camp Lee, Virginia (near Petersburg) in September 1917. Enlistees of the 80th Division were mostly draftees from Virginia, West Virginia and the western counties of Pennsylvania (thereby being designated the "Blue Ridge Division"). The majority of the members of the 80th left Hoboken aboard the *Leviathon* on May 22, arriving in Brest on May 30 . Actions seen by these men included combat, alongside the British, in the Artois Sector (July 23), followed by the Somme Offensive, St. Mihiel, and the Meuse-Argonne. The return trip home for most was aboard the *Maui* to Newport News on May 21, 1919.

Lt. Arthur Ashby Grove and Page's Men of the 29th Division in WWI Article of 6/19/2003

While the role of the 80th Division in WW1 was recalled in the last article, the role of a number of Page County's Doughboys in the 29th Division can be a little more detailed for two reasons. First, Lt. Arthur Ashby Grove left a very detailed questionnaire from WW1. Secondly, we have the wonderful opportunity, in the next few articles, to follow him and many men of his command, through letters that he sent his parents during the war. For that reason I need to slightly delay the story of the 29th Division in WW1. But if you look closely, you will note that Grove's military life does trace what was the lineage of what became part (at least the Page County segment) of the 29th Division during WW1.

Nevertheless, first a little about the man . . . as taken, in part, from his obituary.

"The son of John William Grove and Laura Anne Brumback, he was born April 5th, 1883 at the White House on the Shenandoah River about three miles west of Luray where his father was conducting a mercantile business. Two years later in 1885 the family moved to Luray where the firm of Grove and Bro. was organized and later became the most flourishing mercantile business in the county." While the mercantile business would dominate most of A.A. Grove's life, the role of the military was also a major aspect. The son of a member of Co. E, 35th Battalion Virginia Cavalry, C.S.A., Grove grew up in an era where discussion of the Civil War, by the actual men who served in the ranks, was a very real part of life. Perhaps influenced in part by a sense of duty passed on to him by his father, young Arthur first initiated himself into a military environment by attended Luray Military Academy, under "command" of principal James Horace Morrison, a VMI (1860) graduate and a Confederate veteran. Apparently completing his education at Luray High School, Grove went on to attend Roanoke College by 1900. Two years later, on September 9, 1902, Arthur enlisted with the Page Riflemen, also known as Company C, 72nd Virginia Infantry (National Guard).

The Page Riflemen were often quite the center of social activities and, for one example, in July 1904, the company, "along with the Warren Light Infantry as their guests, took part in the celebration of the 43rd anniversary of the Battle of First Manassas held there under the auspices of the Rosser-Gibbons Camp, Confederate Veterans. The exercises consisted of a procession through the town in which the veterans, military companies and the fire department participated, and of speaking and singing in the beautiful park opposite the depot. Late in the afternoon the companies drilled on the lawn and the Page Riflemen engaged in target practice. An excellent lunch and supper were served the visiting military by the ladies of Rosser-Gibbons Camp."

In the fall of 1908, Grove took advantage of a rarely utilized advantage found deep within the laws of the Commonwealth. In his WW1 questionnaire, he noted that he was the "only officer in the Virginia National Guard who ever took advantage of the provision in the Va. Code that allows any officer of the Va. NG to take a course of instruction at the Virginia Military Institute."

Arthur Ashby Grove,
the Mexican Border Crisis and the Coming of WWI
Article of 7/3/2003

When we last left Arthur Ashby Grove, he was in the midst of beginning a long and active service in the Virginia National Guard. However, in the meantime, he did not let his role in public service go without attention. In August 1906, Arthur was among those to organize and become the first lieutenant commander of the local Summers-Koontz Camp No. 490, Sons of Confederate Veterans, chartered just a month later in Luray. Additionally, among other things including his responsibilities as a partner in the Grove and Brothers Store, on February 28, 1913, Arthur, along with several other future WW1 veterans including Col. R.F. Leedy and C.G. Mason, met at Luray High School and were among those to form Troop 7 of the Boy Scouts of America. Arthur was the first to be appointed Scoutmaster that same year and was succeeded by Rev. C.J. Gibson in 1914.

By 1916, A.A. Grove's involvement in Luray affairs was winding down for a while. Things were coming to a crucial point in the U.S. involvement in the most recent world affairs. With the Mexican Border Crisis, the Page Rifles were activated, along with the balance of the 2nd Virginia Regiment and many other National Guard units, in 1916. On June 28, 1916, Lt. Grove wrote from Richmond that he had "just been examined and passed o.k. for which I am very glad. They were not so strict on the field and staff as they were on the companies . . . All of the Luray crowd passed. Albert Chapman, Tom Holtzman, Elwood Campbell and Shoemaker are in Co. D Front Royal, Capt. Waller. Andrews is in Co. C. Warrenton, Capt. Wood. Bernard Dyche is in Co. D but is detailed as Headquarters Clerk. John Leedy and Peachy Menefee are Color-Sgts." Grove continued, "My job as Inspector of Small Arms Practice ends July 1st. . . Col. Leedy has been good enough to assign me to the Machine Gun Co. which will be recruited. [C.G.] Mason is a very busy man. He is a fine adjutant."

As Arthur closed his letter to his mother, he included "Now don't worry about me. I am going to take care of myself. If we do have war, which I believe we will, I am going to try to do my duty and I hope I can make as good a soldier as they all said Papa was."

Interestingly, he included a "P.S." wherein he spoke of many refusing to take the oath of foreign service. However, all in the Luray company took the oath. By July, the company was on its way to Brownsville, Texas, where they would remain for several months.

Arthur wrote often of weather that was unusual to a man from the Shenandoah Valley but also spoke of long Marches, or "hikes" as he described them. News from home was also reflected in Grove's letters including mention of the Grove Brothers Store and the "pending RR strike" and the hopes that it did not "hold up deliveries of fall goods." Arthur also wrote, "If the 8 hour labor law passes it may bring the RR shop to Luray."

By November, Grove wrote happily of the election of Woodrow Wilson and mentioned that the men in the regiment could no longer be called "tin soldiers" anymore as they had faced "everything but bullets."

From Brownsville to Brest – Page County Men in WWI
Article of 7/17/2003

As we continue to follow the majority of the Page County men in the ranks in 1917, most serving in the 2nd Virginia Infantry at the time, we see that they left Brownsville, Texas by February 1917 and, for a while were able to rejoin family and friends at home. However, time at home was again cut short when on March 25, 1917, the regiment was again inducted into regular service in response to the call from President Wilson. Records show that the regiment was actually mobilized at Staunton on March 30, 1917. Only a few days later, on April 6, the *Page News & Courier* reported the declaration of war against Germany. The men of the 116th from Luray left on April 15 for Roanoke.

Initially placed on guard duty at railroad bridges at Natural Bridge from April to Aug 26, 1917, the 2nd Regt. was again mobilized at Roanoke and, by September 6, 1917, had arrived at Camp McClellan, Anniston, Alabama for an extensive period of training. Within a month, the 1st, 2nd and 4th Virginia Regiments were combined to form the 116th Infantry Regiment (also taking the name Stonewall Brigade as a point of military lineage) that, in turn, was assigned to the 29th Infantry Division. Because this division was made up of units from Virginia, Maryland and Pennsylvania, New Jersey, Delaware and the District of Columbia and had lineal ties to both Union and Confederate units from the American Civil War, the 29th was also called the "Blue and Gray Division."

Lt. Arthur Ashby Grove wrote by November that the men of the 116th were digging trenches and beginning life to prepare them for trench warfare overseas. Grove wrote that he had no doubt that "we are going across." "Papa took his chance in the Civil War and I am willing to take mine in this. If not it is all right as I would just as leave go this way as any other and if I do I feel like it will balance up . . . It is a just cause and I am proud to be an officer in the U.S. Army."

Capt. Charles T. Holtzman, Jr. also made comments about life while at Camp McClellan saying that it was "far below par." Holtzman continued that "We were only trained in discipline and physically and in Civil War Tactics. Very few of our men saw an automatic rifle or live grenade or had any idea of formations for a modern attack until a few weeks before going into attack."

One of Grove's last letters before heading "over there" was on April 13, 1918 when he mentioned that he hoped that there was "no more Pro-German talk in Page Co. . . . The people ought to put a stop to it and they will when the country is aroused." Less than two months later, the 116th pulled out of Camp McClellan and traveled to the Port of Embarkation at Hoboken, NJ.

By that time, a number of Page County men had already made their way to France. As early as April, 1918, Clarence W. Gochenour of Co. A, 2nd Bttn., 3rd Division, was among the first from the county to set off from Newport News aboard the *Altona*. Within days, regular army officer Edward Mallory Almond set off aboard the *Acquatania*. On May 16, Leo C. Bradley of the 320th Inf., 80th Division set off from Newport News aboard the *Mercury* while, six days later, on May 22 several Page men in the 318th Inf., 80th Div., including Samuel D. Price and Hubert Monroe Strickler, set off from Hoboken aboard the *Leviathon*.

While there were many more yet to make the voyage in the coming months, the bulk of Page County men, from the 116th Infantry, set off from Hoboken aboard the *Finland* in mid-June and arrived at St. Nazaire, France on the evening of June 27.

By June 1918, Page County had a considerable number of her "sons" in the field ready for combat duty. Not since the American Civil War, over 50 years before, had the county seen so many of its men ready to step into harm's way.

The War to End all Wars: Page Goes to France
Article of 7/31/2003

Before Page's sons set foot in France in 1918, the county had suffered its first losses of the war. Franklin A. Eppard was the first recorded to have died of illness, followed by Isaac Aleshire in March 1918 of pneumonia. Thomas C. Brubaker and Charles C. Wood would follow, also from pneumonia, before any combat casualties were recorded among the men of Page. By the close of the war, pneumonia would prove the cause of deaths, second only to combat wounds.

From their arrival in France, service strictly amongst fellow American units was not the standard for Page men. A handful of veterans in their questionnaires recorded that they had served alongside (and even integrated at times) with the French, British and Polish troops. By July 1918, Page men had been exposed to enemy fire in at various points including fighting at Chezy, July 18; in the Center Section on July 20; Aveluy Wood on July 22; Artois Sector and St. Mihiel, July 23; and the Houte Alsace (center section), July 25. In turn, the first combat fatalities were recorded within the same month with the deaths of William Seekford, Daniel F. Southard (July 18), and William C. Yancey (July 26). As the combat intensified over the next two months, in addition to the places mentioned for July, Page men also saw action at places such as Balschwiller, Meuse-Argonne, and Verdun. Ray H. Stover, Robert L. Sours and Walter E. Campbell accounted for the three Page men killed in action from August to September.

While the casualty count continued to grow as the weeks went by, on the night of October 9, 1918, an enemy artillery shell falling amongst Lt. Arthur A. Grove's unit proved the single most disastrous day in the history of Page in World War I. Elwood Campbell, Julian R. Campbell and Julian Miller were all severely wounded in the explosion, subsequently resulting in the deaths of all three men. Grove wrote to his parents "A lot of men were in a dug out and a shell made a direct hit on it. Four men were killed and a number wounded. George Vogt was in the same dugout but was not hurt, except shell shock. I had him sent to the hospital."

Another letter from Lt. Grove to his parents on October 26, 1918 may have accurately reflected the thoughts and experiences by many at that time of the war. "All have been thinking a lot of our mothers and fathers," wrote Grove. "I believe I have fallen off at least 20 lbs. . . . my britches are 4 or 5 in. too large in the waist. . . . If anyone had told me that I could stand what I have, I would not have believed him. A man can stand anything he had to. I feel the Lord has been with me."

Though constant word of peace talks were circulated in the ranks, the men could not see any hope of it in the daily fighting and gassings. Lt. Grove's questionnaire gave insight into the daily routine during the month of October . . . "The company was attached to the 2nd Bttn. 116th Inf., and started in the Argonne Drive on the morning of Oct 6, between Samogneux and Brabant, about 15 km North of Verdun. In action on Oct 8 defense center sector Haute Alsace in action at Malbrouck Hill, 10/8; Molleville Farm, Oct. 10; Bois d'Ormont, Oct 11; Grande Montagne, Oct 16; Etraye Ridge, Oct 23; Bois Belleu, Oct 26." "We have been under the Hun shell fire ever since the 8th and they have shelled us every day," wrote Grove to his parents. Last night they hit our dugout and filled it with shell smoke. They also threw over some gas shells – sneezing gas which is very unpleasant. We have to get our masks on in a hurry. Our gas masks and steel helmets are our best friends." Near the close of his letter, he made the point that, "As I said before there is nothing romantic about modern warfare. No flags, no band."

While peace did in fact come within two weeks, there would also be an intensity in the fighting that would continue to take a toll on the men in the trenches.

Nearing the End
&
The 11th Hour of the 11th Day of the 11th Month
Article of 8/14/2003

By the end of October 1918, Page County had tallied up several more casualties in the war to end all wars. However, as with most early wars, more were dying of sickness than of bullets and bombs. By the time Lt. Arthur Ashby Grove had addressed a long letter to his family on October 26, 1918, the Allied forces had made significant progress in defeating the Germans. As evidence of the advance, the letter had been "written in about four different former German dugouts." Reflecting on the action of October 23 at Bois Belleu, Grove wrote, "We made another advance . . . and I am truly thankful that I came out all right. The Lord was certainly with me that day. I never was shot at so often before. Three of the poor fellows in our Co. were killed and 13 wounded and why our losses were not greater is due to the mercy of the Lord alone. Our attack commenced at 6:15 a.m. It was preceded by a 45 minute barrage from our artillery. It was awful. When the barrage lifted we advanced. We had only two platoons left in our Co., one under Sgt. Hunt followed the first line and I followed the second wave with the rest of the Co. The first wave went over without much trouble but the second wave was shot into by some Boche [German] machine gun nests and we had a rather hard time of it. . . The worst part of it was the wounded. We just couldn't get them back until after dark as the Huns had us spotted and every time a man raised his head he drew fire."

As rumors began to float about that the Germans were possibly seeking terms of surrender, Page men still continued to fall in battle. Within the first week of November Charles Grimsley, Homer B. Jenkins, Andrew J. Burner, William C. Burrill, and Floyd Lucas were killed. Despite tragic losses, the spirits of the men were still good. "We continue to hear good news from all fronts," wrote Grove, "Austria wants to quit and probably has, Turkey has enough and I am sure Germany can't hold out much longer. I am glad we got here in time to help save some though I am sorry we have lost the men we have."

On November 9, 1918, two days before the surrender, the last two men from Page County arrived in France from Hoboken, N.J. At the eleventh hour of the eleventh day of the eleventh month of 1918, it all finally came to an end. The cost in men lost (24) from Page County had been significant for a war where their participation had, in essence, only been for five months. Though the war had come to an end, a quick return home was not in the cards for the men. A great majority of the men from Page County, according to postwar questionnaires, arrived back in the States in the spring of 1919 and were discharged by May. However, some did not return as early and were not discharged until as late as August 1919.

Arthur Ashby Grove and his Work after WW1
Article of 8/28/03

In a letter written in December 1918 from France, just less than a month after the conclusion of the war, Lt. Grove wrote that he hoped that "this will be the last Christmas I will have to be away from home as that is one time that I want to be home. Am quite sure it will be the last I shall spend in the army. The War is over and the sooner they send me home the better I shall be pleased. All of the officers were asked to express their wishes as to whether they wanted to go into the regular army, officer's reserve or wanted prompt and final separation from the service. It did not take me long to decide that I want to go to Luray, Va."

Unfortunately the request would take several more months to fulfill. Moving about in France for the next few months, the tedium of the wait no doubt wore on Lt. Grove. While in Nice, France on March 2, 1919, Grove had perhaps the third known photograph of himself taken during the war. Finally, on May 10, 1919, Grove and several Page County men of the 116th Infantry of the 29th Division set sail for home on May 10 aboard the *Matsonia*. Nearly three weeks later at Camp Lee, Grove received his discharge.

Grove's return to civilian life soon resumed with his continued partnership with his brother, Harry E. Grove, in running the Grove and Bro. mercantile store (now the Luray Copy Center) in Luray. However, Grove was not content to rest with his business alone. As with before the war, he continued his participation in the Summers-Koontz Camp No. 490, Sons of Confederate Veterans and participated in many new civic organizations. According to his obituary, "No man in the history of Page County has a broader record of civic interest." Organizations and projects to which Grove had immediate ties included the Shenandoah National Park, the Lee Highway, the Luray Merchants Association, the Luray Rotary Club (of which he was the third president from 1929-30), the Luray Park Board, the past adjutant and commander of the Miller-Campbell Post of the American Legion, the Luray Chamber of Commerce, and the Board of Directors of the Page Valley National Bank of Luray."

On August 14, 1940 Grove fell critically ill and despite all efforts to resuscitate him and despite his being in best of spirits believing he would overcome his illness, Grove died on Wednesday, August 21. His death was a direct result of a heart attack brought on by "physical infirmities resulting from gas received in the World War." In his obituary of August 23, the *Page News & Courier*" noted that his death "filled this community and this section of Virginia with a sorrow and sense of loss seldom experienced." His funeral at Green Hill Cemetery ended with "a regular army firing squad" delivering a 21-gun salute over the grave, followed by the sounding of "Taps." His service to country and his community identified himself as a true model of Cincinattus . . . the Roman general and citizen-soldier who preferred to return to his farm instead of staying in power.

Many, many thanks to Mrs. Ann Vaughn who gave so freely of information that she had about family member, Arthur Ashby Grove.

A Forgotten Symbol of Sacrifice:
The Bronze Tablet Memorial to Page's WW1 Dead
Article of 3/4/2004

On August 7, 1928, approximately 5,000 spectators from throughout the county descended on Luray and lined the streets to take part in the day's events. Despite the heavy downpour that afternoon, few seemed to be dissuaded from coming out for the parade of veterans and the unveiling of the bronze tablet in honor of the twenty-three (though there were twenty-four) Page County servicemen who were killed or died of other causes during World War I.

The parade lined up at the Luray Caverns Park and the "marching column was headed by the speakers in automobiles, then came boys on ponies, and the half dozen Confederate veterans. Two hundred girls and children in white, carrying French and American flags, the American Legion Auxiliary, the Girl Scouts, county and town officials, Luray Concert Band, Monticello Guards of Charlottesville dressed in Colonial uniforms, American Legion and other ex-service men and Boy Scouts." Additionally, "twenty-five or more veterans" of the Stewart Comer Post from Shenandoah were also in line of march, accounting for nearly all of its membership "which had been in full cooperation with the Luray Legion in promoting the memorial."

In addition to the many guest from throughout the state, the event hosted "scores of visiting ex-service men from Waynesboro, Front Royal, Harrisonburg, Charlottesville and other points, with the Governor of Virginia [Byrd], General S. Gardner Waller, veteran and present commander of the Virginia National Guard, Congressman Thomas W. Harrison, Captain John Paul, John J. Wicker, of Richmond, past commander of the State American Legion, Count de Sartiges, Charge D'Affaires, of the French Embassy, Washington, D.C., and Rev. Dennis Whittle, who was a British soldier in the ill-starred Gallipolis campaign." Gen. John J. Pershing, the American Commander-in-chief, sent a note of regret that he could not be present and participate "in the emotions of his former comrades."

As the parade made its way to the Luray Caverns, people took refuge from the summer deluge amongst the buildings and sheds made specifically for the accommodation of the thousands anticipated at the event. Beginning with Denver Aleshire, commander of the Miller-Campbell post, calling for an invocation from Rev. Whittle, a number of speeches were made before Capt. Wicker unveiled the bronze tablet. Measuring five feet high by three feet wide, the tablet was then borne to the Cathedral Hall in the Caverns by four members of the Miller-Campbell Post and four members of the Stewart Comer Post. Many of the speakers referred to the uniqueness of the monument being placed in the Caverns.

Both Gov. Byrd and the Charge D'Affaires, of the French Embassy concluded the day's events with stirring tributes to Page's fallen sons as well taking the normal liberties of the time to recall the days of the American Revolution when France came to the aid of the American Colonies.

Post World War I Military

A Page County Man on the Yangtze River Patrols, Part 1 (1928) Article of 4/1/2004

Perhaps one of the most entertaining experiences one can have is that of imparting a "sea story" from a sailor. With just the right sailor (with just enough "salt" behind his ears to prove his story of worth) and the right story, you can feel the very ocean fall and rise in every word. Even so, a sea story doesn't always have to be imparted by a person but can prove equally as interesting in the photos, cut-outs, and memorabilia left in a well-kept scrapbook. One such scrapbook passed along to me – a fourth generation of the US Naval service - forms the basis of this article.

It was a time between wars, but the American interests in China held the Navy in an active role there. As Rear Admiral Kemp Tolley pointed out in his book *Yangtze Patrol: The U.S. Navy in China*, the patrols were a "logical result of increasing American commerce with China after the opening of the clipper ship era." Though the USS *Susquehanna* was sent to China as early as 1854, the first regular operations on the Yangtze River began in 1866 when the USS *Monocacy* and USS *Ashuelot* began patrolling the river. Interestingly, the USS *Shenandoah* was one of the ships that came later on that year to reinforce the patrol. Inevitably, these patrols would be the beginning of the longest uninterrupted U.S. Naval operation in history.

One Page County man, Clyde Edward Emerson, the son of an employee of the Norfolk and Western train yards in Shenandoah experienced a taste of life on the Yangtze from 1928 – 1934. The scrapbook outlining his "adventures" in the Far East also gave some indication that he may have had some foresight into service in the Navy through the memories passed on to him by an uncle, Charles Benton Emerson, who had served in the U.S. Navy around the time of the Spanish-American War.

In the spring of 1928, Emerson began his long trek to the orient, taking the U.S.S. *Nitro* and the U.S.S. *Helena*. Stopping briefly in

Guantanamo Bay, Cuba, his journey continued to Nicaragua, the Panama Canal Zone and then on to San Diego, California when he actually began the journey across the Pacific in July 1928. Later that same month, as a crewmember aboard the U.S.S. *Henderson*, he arrived in Hawaii before continuing on to Guam and Midway Island and finally Shanghai, China in August. In October, he was transferred and became a crewmember of the U.S.S. *Tutuila*.

The *Tutuila* (designated PR-4 as a river gunboat) had just come into service (July 1928) on the Yangtze Patrol after having been laid down in the shipyards at Shanghai. According to a website, the *Tutuila* was well designed for the Yangtze. *Tutuila*'s "shallow draft enabled her to traverse the treacherous rapids of the gorges with ease, so that the fluctuating water levels did not hinder her year-round access to the upper stretch of the Yangtze. Her duty with YangPat offered excitement and variety: conducting roving armed patrols; convoying merchantmen; providing armed guards for American flag steamers; and 'showing the flag' to protect American lives and property in a land where civil strife and warfare had been a way of life for centuries."

For those who are familiar with it, a 1966 movie titled "The Sand Pebbles" (starring Steve McQueen and others) gave a glimpse into life on the YangPat (Yangtze Patrol) in the 1920s.

A Page County Man on the Yangtze River Patrols, Part 2 (1929 – 1930) Article of 4/8/2004

While I mentioned that the USS *Tutuila*'s time in service was between wars, the US Navy did not pass the time without military involvement. Having transferred aboard the USS *Tutuila* in October 1928, Clyde Emerson was not long in seeing action.

As a contemporary website reveals, the American gunboats had to deal with "sniping by bandits or warlord troops" that "required both tact and (upon occasion) a few well-placed rounds of 3-inch or .30 caliber gunfire." Writing hastily in his log for November 7, Emerson wrote that they were "fired on below Chunking – returned fire – no casualties – Red Territory." Similar entries followed in weeks to come.

One incident in 1929 involving the USS *Tutuila*, as the aforementioned website describes, "called for a mixture of diplomacy and force . . . when Lt. Comdr. S. D. Truesdell was in command of the gunboat. He called on the Chinese warlord from whose territory some rifle shots had come. During a discussion of the incident, the [Chinese] general explained that his men were merely "country boys, who meant no harm." Truesdell replied that he, too, had some "country boys:" among his own crew. He noted that he had found them tinkering with the after 3-inch gun, pointing it at the general's conspicuous white headquarters, as they practiced their range finding. Truesdell's rejoinder bore immediate fruit; the sniping ceased forthwith!"

Two years later, little had seemed to change on the patrols and Emerson had an opportunity to fully explain life as it was for patrols on the Yangtze. "Guess you have been reading in the papers about trouble on the Yangtze?" wrote Emerson on November 18, 1930. "Well we are anchored in the bandit-infested area for the night. We can only navigate the river in the daytime as we only carry day pilots. Here is what happened today, just to give you some idea of the river life. I had the 12-4 watch last night which I stood with two forty-fives, gats and a searchlight. Had breakfast at 7:30 then took over the 8-10 wheel-watch (The reason for all the watches is we are short of men as we have an armed guard off the ship, on one of the Standard Oil Steamers which is in Hankow at present). At 9:30 we were fired on from the beach with a field piece, which we answered with three-inch machine guns firing four rounds of shrapnel and fifteen rounds of three-inch service ammunition. The fire was silenced on the beach. We secured from general quarters. At 10 o'clock we were fired on again with some kind of a muzzle loader believed to be a field piece, which we answered with five hundred rounds of thirty-thirty (Lewis machine guns) and rive rounds of three inch service ammunition. We had quite a bit of practice today. The gunners mate was supposed to have the wheel but as we only have on aboard, he had to clean the guns. So, I was detailed to take the wheel from 11 to chow. Not much excitement during the afternoon. Was manning #4 Lewis about 4 o'clock when a bandit on the beach raised his gun to fore but seeing our guns take a bearing on him he immediately changed his mind. No more fun today. Had chow at 5 o'clock. Relieved the wheel immediately after chow, and brought the ship to anchor. So ends the day."

The conclusion of Yangtze Patrol life for one Page County man and the fate of the USS *Tutuila* to come next week.

A Page County Man on the Yangtze River Patrols, Part 3 (1930 – 1931) Article of 4/15/2004

While "clashes" on the Yangtze were usually without harm to American sailors, it wasn't always the case. In one event recorded in November 1930, Emerson noted that the USS *Guam* and *Palos* "were shot up wounding five men on the *Palos* and killing one man on the *Guam* . . . the man on the *Guam* was a very close friend of mine. We came through training together, were shipmates on the USS *Nitro* and *Henderson*. Also the USS *Helena*. His name was Elkins, S. The *Tutuila* took his body to Shanghai where it was placed on one of the Dollar steamers for further transportation to the United States." Reviewing the past year, Emerson also noted that the Yangtze Patrol had lost "one man in battle, five enlisted men were wounded, one officer. Five men have been lost in the river; two of which were never seen again. The Japanese, French and English have been fired on as well as the American ships having as many casualties if not more."

While life was certainly trying on the Yangtze Patrols, Emerson obviously (according to the clippings in his scrapbook) was able to enjoy a little onboard "liberty" with readings of the old *Asiatic Fleet Magazine* and when other time permitted, "shore leave" while in the Orient. Clippings relating to visits to the theatre, the Chungking International Race Club, the Naval Canteen at Kiukiang, and a number of old beer labels (interestingly, many of them German) grace the pages of the scrapbook.

A little military competition from time to time didn't hurt either as is seen in a two-page write-up by Emerson explaining a "bull-shoot" competition between the *Tutuila* and the H.M.S. *Peterel*. While the first part of the match seemed pretty bleak for the *Tutuila*, in time the Americans got the edge over the Royal Navy. During the final and deciding phase, bringing to bear a rapid-fire match – "'Mo' Mawhorter, 'Hack' Branan, 'Swede' Gulliksen, and 'Whitey' Whitecotton" pulled through for the *Tutuila*. "It was a darn good match" wrote Emerson, "the winning of which was made more gratifying considering the ability and good sportsmanship of our most worthy opponents."

Though his time with the Navy extended beyond 1931, Emerson recorded nothing in the log beyond that year. However, the USS *Tutuila* continued to serve in the Yangtze and, by 1937, was caught in the middle of the undeclared Sino-Japanese War. Well before Pearl Harbor, the USS *Panay* (a sister ship of the *Tutuila*) was attacked by Japanese aircraft and sunk on Dec. 12, 1937. Bottling-up American ships on the Yangtze, Japanese operations left the *Tutuila* stranded at Chungking through 1941. On July 31 of that same year, the *Tutuila* was attacked by Japanese aircraft and was severely damaged. As one of the two ships left in China when the YangPat was decommissioned on (interestingly) December 6, 1941, the *Tutuila* was decommissioned on January 18, 1942 – the same day that her remaining two officers and 22 men flew out of Chungking. Though the *Tutuila* was officially removed from the Navy logs on March 26, 1942, it was turned over to the Chinese government, continuing service under the name *Mei Yuan* (meaning "of American origin") through the Second World War and, served in the Nationalist Navy through 1948 when she was scuttled to prevent being captured by Communist forces advancing on Shanghai.

Surnames and Genealogical Research Tools

"But What Does It Have to Do with Me?" A Primer in Genealogical Connections
Article of 1/24/02

I've done several articles on different families in the past four years and I have plans to do several more. However, in retrospect, I wonder how many take a look at a particular surname in the title of an article and think – "well, this one has nothing to do with my family." Ironically, if your family has resided in Page County for a fair amount of time, it very well may have something to do with your family tree.

It is interesting to see how, over the course of over 270 years , how many families are actually linked to each other in Page County. Three-quarters of my ancestry has ties to the Page Valley even before it began to carry that name. In the course of speaking with most of my friends in the county, especially when we begin to talk about our roots, we find that we may have at least one common ancestral tie.

Which leads me to begin the prelude for a multi-part article that is to follow over the next several weeks.

First, the article will be largely based on the rarest find for a genealogist. While we all know or most of us have heard of our immigrant ancestors, it is likely that we don't know a fraction of their complete story. We may know the name of our immigrant ancestors, the ship upon which they traveled, the country that they left – even the city-state that they left; but how often do we know the FULL story of their trials in leaving the mother country and the trip across the ocean – especially if it took place over 260 years ago?

Though the two immigrant families upon which I focus did not write the accounts that I will use, they were written by people that either witnessed their departure from the old country, or were in the company of those future progenitors of two Page County families – the Rothgeb/Roadcap and Good families.

It all begins with a 1920 publication of the Pennsylvania German Society. In this publication, the Rev. William John Hinke, Ph.D., D.D. (Professor of Semitic Languages and Religions of Auburn Theological Seminary, Auburn, N.Y.) wrote of the history of the Goshenhoppen Reformed Charge in Montgomery County, Pennsylvania. Specifically, Part XXIX, Chapter III of this publication covered the ministry of John Henry Goetschy from 1735 to 1740, including the trials of his ministry's journey from Switzerland.

Among the many resources that Hinke used were three particularly wonderful finds. The first was the Oct. 7, 1734 issue of the Zurich newspaper that followed the departure of Goetschy's ministry from Switzerland. The second was the pamphlet that was written in 1735 by Goetschy emigrant Ludwig Webber (the only known copy is in existence in the city library in Zurich). The last being an actual letter written in July 1735 by 17 year-old John Henry Goetschy, Jr.

While following only two families that settled in our county, their accounts give us quite an understanding of what so many of our 18th century immigrant ancestors experienced. While I will quote heavily from the actual accounts, I will also interject information that has been passed down through generations that complement the story. I hope that you will join me in experiencing this amazing tale over the next several weeks.

Incidentally, to reach these Good and Rothgeb ancestors in my own family tree, I had to go back seven and eight generations respectively.

Tracing a Given Name May be Just as Interesting as Tracing Surnames Article of 9/2/2004

In the "genealogical pursuit of happiness" sometimes researchers concentrate on one thing so hard that they miss the wealth of information that can be embodied in other things. I've known some researchers to limit their search to the lineage of the father or strictly the male lines. Obviously, if they take the time to search all lines genealogical research can be twice as rewarding. One thing that I realized not long ago was that a search of a given name could yield just as many wonderful surprises.

With each succeeding generation, we give our children names that may or may not tie into familial lineage. Often we see persons naming children for the parents or even grandparents or maybe even great-grandparents. However, in some cases, we may lose sight of just how far back a name may go.

Giving the example of my own name - being a "Robert H. Moore, II", I took the opportunity to name my son "Robert H. Moore, III" just like many have done with their own names in different families over the years. So, my son's name mirrored my own name; my name mirrored that of my father's; my father's name mirrored my grandfather's name in part (my grandfather's middle name was the variable) but mirrored my great-grandfather's name exactly. To that point, it seemed like that was the beginning of the line of Roberts in my family. However, with some revealing research in recent years, I uncovered something that enabled me to trace the name back at least nine generations from my own son.

After all was said and done, at the very least, in my family, the name "Robert" has a clear lineage that can be traced, so far, back to the year 1744. The name "Robert" did not originate with the Moore line, but with the Quigley family from Ireland. In 1744, while living near Quigley's Bridge, Cumberland Co. Pa., James and Jeanette Quigley had a son named Robert Quigley. Interestingly, for many generations, the name Robert was not passed down through the male lines, but through the efforts made by daughters in naming their children. It was not passed down through the male line until it reached the Moore family through my great-great-great grandmother giving it to one of her sons in the 1850s. Regretfully, I am unable to trace James Quigley's parentage and possibly find even more generations of Roberts.

"Robert" Quigley (first known named "Robert") had a daughter named Dinah (born in Cumberland Co., Pa. in 1776), who married Joseph McKinney. Joseph and Dinah, had a son, "Robert" McKinney, born ca. 1811 in Cumberland Co., Pa., who was named for Dinah's father, "Robert" Quigley.

"Robert" McKinney had a daughter, Kate or Catherine A. McKinney, born ca. 1829 in Washington Co., Md. Kate married Cyrus Saunders Moore and in the late 1850s they had a set of twins, one who was given the first name "Robert." Both twins died not long after birth. However, John Howard Moore, a later son of Cyrus and Kate (and the first Moore from my line of Moores to settle in Page County), continued the tradition of the given name "Robert."

John Howard Moore, born in Clear Spring, Washington Co., Md. in 1862, married Mary Davison. Their last child was born in Page County, Virginia in 1896 and named "Robert" Hume Moore – my great-grandfather and who I had believed for many years before to have been the beginning of the "Robert" naming tradition.

So, citing my own line of "Robert" as an example, be sure to take the time to research your given names as well and perhaps you may have the opportunity to enjoy genealogy through a different light other than just the tracing of the surnames.

An Early Record of the Life of Doctor Thomas Benjamin Amiss Article of 3/13/2003

In 1874, Thomas Benjamin Amiss, a Rappahannock County physician, found his way to Page County and initially settled in Alma to begin a long and popular reign as one of the county's finest doctors. Though the memory of the once famous county doctor is fading from the memory of succeeding generations, the name of Doctor Amiss sat fondly in the thoughts of those who knew the man.

Born at "Melville" in Amissville on July 4, 1839, T.B. Amiss was a son of Elijah and Ann Elizabeth Leavell Amiss. In the mid 1850s, Amiss matriculated at the Virginia Military Institute (Class of 1859/60) from Peola Mills, Madison County, Virginia. However, he remained for only three years before moving on to the University of Pennsylvania where he obtained his medical degree in March 1861. Though Virginia was soon amidst the decisions of secession and ultimately cast her lot with the Confederacy, Amiss moved ahead with plans to open his practice in Virginia.

However, the war inevitably called for Amiss' services. Interestingly, at least four sources give conflicting stories of his service at the beginning of the war. In piecing all of the different accounts together, initially it appears that, in lieu of performing medical service, he was also involved in "putting in practice instead the lessons he had learned in Lexington, drilling the volunteer companies of Rappahannock and Culpeper Counties." Another account reflects that by September 1861, he was assigned as assistant surgeon at Bailey's Factory Hospital in Richmond. Though it seems odd that a physician with skills in high demand would be called to enlist, on April 1, 1862 he was, in fact, recorded as having enlisted as a corporal in Co. B, 6th Virginia Cavalry. However, within a month, owing to the fact that he was a physician, he was recorded as absent on detached service with the Medical Department in Richmond.

By the summer of 1862, his services were clearly needed in the field and he was assigned as surgeon of the 31st Georgia Infantry. He continued to serve with this regiment from the Battle of Cedar Mountain in August 1862 through to the Battle of Chancellorsville in May 1863. At that time, due to impaired health, Amiss was assigned to hospital duty and ordered to report to a Dr. Curry at Salisbury, N.C. When the Salisbury garrison was transferred to Camp Sumter at Andersonville, Georgia, Amiss was ordered to report to a Major Webb at Weldon, N.C., where he remained until the surrender of Gen. Joseph E. Johnston's Army of the Tennessee, when he was paroled.

Following the war, Amiss returned to Virginia and set up his practice in Slate Mills in Rappahannock County until 1874. Undoubtedly, this record of service would be fairly adequate in outlining the service of a surgeon in the Civil War. However, Amiss had one particular incident in his service that established his name throughout the field of abdominal surgery. More details on that particular surgery on the Cedar Mountain battlefield in the next article . . .

The Amazing Medical Feat of Dr. T.B. Amiss, Confederate Surgeon, Part 1

Article of 3/27/2003

By August 1862, Dr. Thomas B. Amiss had secured a transfer from his duties at the Bailey's Factor Hospital in Richmond to an assignment as assistant surgeon to the 31st Georgia Infantry of Gen. Alexander R. Lawton's Georgia Brigade; the same brigade as his brother, William, who was with the 60th Georgia Infantry. By August 8, Lawton's Brigade, along with the rest of Jackson's command was preparing for a fight with Federal forces at Cedar Mountain in Culpeper County. Though Lawton's Brigade was placed in the rear to guard the supply trains of Jackson's army, surgeons would still be much in need at the front as the battle opened on the following day.

Late in the afternoon and near an area of intense fighting on the field, artillery Major Snowden Andrews, a Marylander, was directing guns of his battalion when he was severely wounded by an exploding shell which sliced open Andrew's right abdominal wall. Throwing an arm across the gaping wound and while grasping the neck of his horse, the major slid as carefully as he could from the horse to prevent being disemboweled. Artillerists all around Andrews knew at once that the wound must be fatal. However, soon thereafter, Gen. A.P. Hill rode near the spot of Andrew's saw Andrews and promised to send help at the first opportunity. Indeed, within a short time, Doctor Hunter H. McGuire, Stonewall Jackson's staff surgeon, was on the scene assessing Andrews' condition and expressed with a clear bluntness that the artillery major's chances were hopeless. Andrews, having received a similar diagnosis from others replied, "Yes, that's what you fellows all say." Unable to give the major any comfort, McGuire sent for the doctors Amiss.

Dr. T.B. Amiss recalled that early that evening, a courier arrived before him and announced "that Dr. McGuire wanted him to look after a wounded man lying on the roadside." Asking the courier to guide him and his brother to the spot where the wounded officer lay, the party set off and "arrived at a roadside and found the wounded man a few feet inside a field." Amiss dismounted and found the major in a sorry state. Calling back to his brother, Amiss was much more blunt than McGuire and yelled, "the only thing to do to this man is to dig a hole and put him in it." Andrews, with equal degree of response, stated, "That is what Dr. McGuire told me, but if you damn doctors would do something for me, I would get well." Amiss replied in turn, "My friend, do you know that your bowels are all out and covered with hen-grass, clay, dust, and sand?" Andrews again replied, "I had a hound dog run a mile with his guts out, and caught a fox; and I know I am as good as a dog; and can stand as much."

Pulling the blanket back, Amiss discovered that Andrews was a major and exclaimed to William, "This man is full of all sorts of grit (meaning sand from the road and physical stamina as well) and we will do what we can for him."

The Amazing Medical Feat of Dr. T.B. Amiss, Confederate Surgeon, Part 2 Article of 4/10/2003

After realizing that Major Snowden Andrews, despite his severe wound, was "full of all sorts of grit," Dr. Thomas B. Amiss ordered his litter-bearers to carry the major to the nearby farmhouse owned by Mr. James Garnett. The trip to the rear was extremely painful for the major due to the springless ambulance in which he rode. Along the way, a chaplain held the major's hand and recited familiar hymns, likely believing much the same as the doctors, in that Andrews' situation was hopeless. .

At around midnight, the ambulance finally arrived at the Garnett house and the artillery major was carried into the house and placed on the dining table where the doctors Amiss began to do what they could. While Dr. William Amiss washed the abdominal cavity "removing therefrom a handful of sand and vegetable matter," a portion of hipbone was also removed. Dr. T.B. Amiss recalled, "The work was all carefully done, and the washing and sponging was done with salt solution. The sewing up of the wound, about 7 inches long, I did with ordinary Boss cotton and a calico needle." Andrews did what he could through the procedure by holding the wound's edges together. Despite all that could possibly done, another surgeon, Dr. Harvey Black, from the Stonewall Brigade, stopped in to observe and when asked if there was any hope also concurred that there was none.

Following the surgery, Andrews, "perfectly cool and composed, and even cheerful," asked the doctors again of his chances. Receiving no response, he suggested himself aloud that he hoped for at least one chance in ten or twenty. Ultimately, the surgeon replied, "Not more than that." In return, Andrews declared, cheerfully, that he intended to "hold on to my one chance." Just in case, Major Andrews gave to the care of Marylander and friend McHenry Howard, his personal seal ring to deliver to his wife in the event that the worst should happen.

Remarkably, after five weeks, peritonitis had yet to set in and Andrews was finally able to sit up. By the spring of 1863, wearing a silver plate over his wound, Andrews returned to the field and command, as a lieutenant colonel, of a battalion of artillery. Andrews would not die until 1903.

According to an account written many years later by Dr. Amos R. Koontz, "the notoriety of this recovery was freely discussed by the medical fraternity of London just before the breaking out of the Franco-Prussian War, and it was suggested that the recovery was due to dust from the roadside which had completely settled over the wound, and careful surgery afterwards. This led to the practice of dust treatment for wounds in the Franco-Prussian War, and this in turn left to the use of antiseptic powders in wound treatment."

Transferring his practice from Rappahannock County to Page County in 1874, Dr. Thomas B. Amiss' service as a doctor in the community and as a surgeon in the Civil War carried over to an appointment as surgeon of the Rosser-Gibbons Camp, United Confederate Veterans in Luray from its organization in 1898. After almost four decades of service to the citizens of the Page Valley, Dr. Amiss died on November 9, 1913 and rests honored today along with over 85 fellow Confederates in Luray's Green Hill Cemetery.

General Turner Ashby's Ties to Page County
Article of 7/15/2004

While he was known for his service in the Shenandoah Valley as Stonewall Jackson's chief cavalryman, Turner Ashby was known for other things in the Valley before the Civil War. A magnificent horseman, Ashby was known as the "Black Knight" before the war specifically for his skill as a jouster, regularly taking part in the jousting tournaments that took place at Natural Chimneys in Augusta County. But, according to the recollections of his first cousin, Dollie Tutt Rhodes, Ashby also had "come-a-courtin'" in Luray on occasion.

Though not the attention of his romantic affections, Dollie Rhodes can be given credit for being the one who conveyed the stories of Ashby and his Page County romance with a Miss Bettie Lionberger. However, the connection with Dollie is interesting as it makes an indirect connection between the general and, at the least, the Rhodes family in Luray. Named partly for her mother's sister (Dollie Ashby), Dorothy "Dollie Maria Tutt (born in Fauquier County on May 15, 1820) married Luray native, A.H. Rhodes (born in 1812). Dolly's mother, Elizabeth "Betsy" Ashby Tutt (wife of Col. John Tutt) was the daughter of Captain John Ashby (1740 – 1815) and Mary Elizabeth Turner as well as a sister to Turner Ashby, Sr., father of the famous General Turner Ashby.

According to the March 26, 1915 issue of the *Page News & Courier*, Dollie, who visited Luray often, could give "many reminiscences of her famous relative, as they were closely associated in childhood. Their homes were not more than half a mile apart at Markham, Fauquier County. As a boy the future cavalry hero of the Valley campaign was noted for his dare-deviltry and his unceasing propensity to mischief. Mrs. Rhodes suffered from some of his pranks and was once almost rolled into a milldam by him. He grew to be a small, dark man resembling a Mexican or Spaniard. He and his younger brother Dick were inseparable. As boys they were expert swimmers and seemed to almost live in the old millrace that ran by their home. Later like the young men of their class in the South they became enthusiastic foxhunters and gave a great deal of time to sports. Turner Ashby was the finest horseback rider in Fauquier County."

According to her sharp memory, even at 95 years of age, Dollie recalled that the last time she had seen Turner was when the Tutt family moved from Virginia to Missouri in the 1830s when she was "about fifteen years old." However, "some years before the war, Ashby came to Missouri to visit his relatives but Mrs. Rhodes did not see him for some cause. One of the attractions that took him to the West was the presence there of Miss Bettie Lionberger." Known "as a beautiful young lady in whom he [Turner Ashby] evinced much interest," Bettie Lionberger was the daughter of Isaac Lionberger, brother of Luray's John Lionberger.

Though he never married, following Bettie Lionberger's return to Luray, according to Dollie Rhodes, "Ashby came to Luray to visit Miss Lionberger" who was at the time living at the brick property now [1915] occupied by W.M. Rosser when Ashby was her guest." (This building still stands on the northeast corner of Hawksbill and Main Streets).

Regretfully, nothing more can be found about the romance between Ashby and Miss Lionberger. There is no mention of a continuing courtship through the early years of the war, but one has to wonder just how close the couple may have been at the time of General Ashby's demise at the Battle of Harrisonburg on June 6, 1862 and how the Lionberger household could have been a focal point of mourning in Luray.

Dollie Rhodes died on May 2, 1917 in San Antonio, Texas.

The Booton/Booten Family and Its Role in Early Page County History, Part 1
Article of 2/5/2004

It appears that the earliest record of the Booton family line of Page County ties in with one Joshua Boughton, born ca. 1680. At least one of his children, William, was born in Culpeper, Culpeper County in 1712. In 1738, William married Judith Hill, the daughter of William and Frances Needles Hill (of Middlesex County). Children of William and Frances included Lewis, Ambrose, Eliza, William, and Ann. Ambrose's line is central in the descendants who followed in Page County.

Like his father, Ambrose lived and died in Culpeper Co. He married Tomagen Rucker (daughter of Ephraim and Margaret Vawter Rucker) ca 1763 and children born to the union included John K., Ambrose, Anna and Elizabeth.

During the American Revolution there were a number of Booton family members who served in various capacities and units including Joshua (3rd, 5th, 7th, and 11th Continental Line), Lewis (Ensign of the Culpeper Militia in 1780), Travis & William (both of the cavalry) and another William who served in the 2nd Continental Line. Another Booton/Booten, Reuben, was listed also as having served.

The oldest child, John K. Booton was born in Madison Co. in 1765 and married Frances Clark in 1786.

Among their children were included Reuben, Abraham, Bathsheba, Ambrose Crittendon, James, William, Elizabeth, Jemima, and Thomason. Of those children, at least three or four eventually settled in the part of Shenandoah County that eventually became Page County.

Ambrose C. Booton (born January 26, 1789) seems to have headlined the group of siblings in Page County. Born in Orange County, he was married on May 9, 1809 to Susannah Fallis, and that union produced several children before she died in 1827 (including John Kaylor Booton, born August 19, 1823). Following the death of his first wife, Ambrose married Elizabeth Fry/Fray Grubb, daughter of John V. Grubb.

On January 10, 1814, Ambrose produced credentials, in Shenandoah County, "of his ordination, and of his being in regular communion with the Hawksbill Baptist Church, gave bond, took the oath of fidelity to the commonwealth, & was licensed to solemnize marriages." Additionally, Ambrose served as postmaster of Long Meadows in Page County as early as 1838 (the post office and village was discontinued by 1856) and played an instrumental role in opening the Luray Female Seminary, over which his son, John K. Booton (named for his grandfather) was principal ca. 1855. On April 7, 1858, Ambrose, his son John K. and William C. Lauck all partnered in incorporating the Luray Institute. Perhaps his most popular role was that of minister of the Mill Creek Church from 1846 until his death on March 29, 1865. His wife, Elizabeth died only a few days later on April 2, 1865 (both Ambrose and Elizabeth died of pneumonia). Both were buried in the Abraham Spitler Cemetery in Mill Creek.

There were a number of Ambrose's siblings who also appeared to have played a role in the early history of Page County, according to census records.

Bathsheba was listed as living with James and Frances Parks in Marksville 1860. Apparently her son was William L. Booton. In 1850 the mother and son were listed as living at the home of Walker Eddins.

Thomason R. Booton, at age 49, was shown as living at the home of Lydia F. Fristoe in Hope Mills in 1860. She died in 1884.

The Booton/Booten Family and Its Role in Early Page County History, Part 2
Article of 2/12/2004

Having established Ambrose C. Booton as one of the forerunners of the Booton family in Page County, Ambrose's children carried the line into generations that continue in Page County today. A.C. Booton's oldest daughter, Letitia, married Frederick A. Marye in 1835 and another daughter, Elizabeth F.M., married David Moncell Dovel in 1842.

John Kaylor Booton (born in 1823), mentioned briefly in the previous article, was a man of various means. Listed as an inventor in the 1860 Page Co. census, he was instrumental in 1861 as the founder and main funding agent behind the Dixie Artillery. In October 1861, Booton was elected to the Virginia State Legislature and resigned his post as captain of the Confederate battery. In addition to his duties as a representative, he was also in charge of the county's harness-making industry (his tannery being destroyed twice by Federal troops) until the end of the war. By 1870, Booton had followed in his father's footsteps and was ordained as a Primitive Baptist Minister. Booton was married to Emily Heiskell Lauck in Feb. 1862 and died Dec. 19, 1903.

A first cousin to J.K. Booton, John Green Booton was another notable Booton of Page County. Born in 1830 to James C. & Lucy Modesitt Booton (daughter of Peter & Eleanor Marye and widow of James W. Modesitt), J.G. Booton graduated from Jefferson Medical School in Philadelphia in 1854 and was soon after a practicing physician in Page County. In 1855, Dr. Booton married Martha A. Lauck, the sister J.K. Booton's future spouse. At the opening of the Civil War, Booton cast his fortunes as surgeon with the Dixie Artillery. However, there is no further record of his service with the battery. Nevertheless, Booton was known as practicing medicine in Virginia until his death in 1896 in Page County.

Other Booton family members listed in Page in the 1860 census were William E. Booton, Sylvanus T. Booton, and Reuben L. Booton.

William Edward Booton (born 1829 in Madison Co., a son of Abraham and Bathsheba Clarke Booton). A member of Co. E, 97th Va. Militia at the opening of the Civil War, William lived in the area that became known as Stanley and was married to Rebecca F. Lucas (d/o of Levi and Ellen Printz Lucas).

Sylvanus T. Booton, (born ca. 1837 in Madison Co., a son of Thornton & Jemima Clift Booton). Married in Page County in 1857 to Mary Jane Cornwell, Sylvanus either enlisted or was conscripted into the ranks of Co. H, 33rd Va. Infantry in September 1862. Within a year, he had deserted, but returned and faced a court martial, which, in the end, found him guilty and sentenced him to stand on a 4-foot block on the regimental color line for 2 hours everyday, for 15 days. Though he was also sentenced with 6 months hard labor, he was unable to complete his punishment and likely contracted the pneumonia that killed him in April 1864, from his winter standings on the color line.

Reuben L. Booton, who served as a member of Co. D, 7th Virginia Cavalry and was perhaps Page's first man killed in the war at Romney on July 12, 1861.

The family name is also a fixture in Page in one of the many smaller gaps that cross the Blue Ridge into the county. According to a local story, the aforementioned, William Edward Booton was actually somewhat responsible for the naming of this gap. "Remembered as a leader in the people of his area in the 'Basin' . . . the U.S. Park Service erected a marker to his memory on the Skyline Drive and the place is called 'Booten's Gap.'"

Brown's Book and Public Discussion on Sam Chapman
Article of 7/11/2002

A few months back, I realized that the above-mentioned book, written by Peter A. Brown and published in 2001, had missed some major publicity as an item of things relevant to the history of Page County.

Indeed, Samuel Forrer Chapman was a native of Page County. The son of William Allen and Elizabeth Forrer Chapman, Sam was born Aug. 27, 1838, at the home of his mother's parents, Samuel and Catherine Forrer, at what most folks know more commonly as the Clark House opposite Willow Grove Mill. Though his postwar life led him to Covington, where he lived and preached for the balance of his life from the 1880s, his rise to fame in the Civil War as one of Mosby's company commanders, was while he was a citizen of Page County.

Peter Brown's book is a fascinating collection of materials that piece the life of Samuel Chapman together. The early history of the Chapman, Forrer, Kendrick, Gaines and Ebersole families as they relate to the history of Page County, is also revealed in a wonderful read by Brown.

Brown also brings to light the affiliation between the Forrer children and the introduction of New York native Jedediah Hotchkiss (Stonewall Jackson's future mapmaker) as a teacher. By 1850, Sam Chapman was among an ever-growing number of Hotchkiss' students and by 1854, Mossy Creek Academy was a facility where many children of wealthy families came to learn the many disciplines, including a handful from Page County.

By 1858, Sam was a student at Columbian College in Washington, D.C., and was inspired by the teachings in the school founded mostly by Baptist ministers from Virginia. On May 2 of that year, as members of the Main Street Baptist Church in Luray, he and his brother William were baptized. Five months later, the congregation passed a resolution that Sam be granted a license to "exercise his gifts in preaching and exhortation to his fellow men." In turn, Sam entered Richmond College as a ministerial student.

While holding the professional title of "minister" by the opening of the war, Chapman would have to put his calling on temporary hold for four years, while he became known as a man of remarkable skill in the saddle. Mosby later wrote of Chapman, "His character as a soldier was more on the model of the Hebrew prophets than the Evangelist or the Baptist in whom he was so devout a believer. He was generally in front of everybody in a fight."

Author Peter Brown will be present at the Luray fire station at 8 p.m. on Thursday, July 18, to talk in detail of Sam Chapman's fascinating life. The program, sponsored by the Summers-Koontz Camp 490, Sons of Confederate Veterans, is free to the public.

The Legacy of Luray Marble Cutter Daniel Fagan
Article of 5/2/2002

Many a car goes past Green Hill Cemetery in Luray, but does everybody know of the man that made the once beautiful Victorian-era cemetery a highly desirable final resting place among so many of Luray's post Civil War society?

Daniel Fagan was a son of Irish parents. Following immigration, while his parents resided for a short time in New York, Daniel was born in 1827. From New York, the Fagan family moved to Winchester, Virginia. Around 1840, John founded the Old Valley Marble Works in Winchester in an inn that he had purchased in 1839. Says a family website – "When he died". . . he was known to "have all the virtues and a few of the vices of the Irish people."

Long before the death of his father, Daniel had taken up the trade of marble cutting. As a well-established professional, Daniel also found time for romance and married Hanna Madison "Mattie" Simpson of Fauquier Co., perhaps sometime in the 1850s.

With the events brought about by John Brown at Harpers Ferry, Daniel, as a member of the Continental Morgan Guards of Winchester, was called to service and was present at Charles Town and the hanging of John Brown. Shortly thereafter, Fagan appears to have made his way to Page County, perhaps to generate a "satellite" for his father's Winchester business.

However, once again, Daniel's work was interrupted with the outbreak of the war. Being well trained with the militia in the military arts, Fagan was involved with the organization of the Page Volunteers (Co. K, 10th Va. Inf.) and was mustered in with the company as 1st lieutenant on June 2, 1861. Just over a month later, Fagan was wounded at the First Battle of Manassas. His wound must have been rather debilitating, as he remained absent from the company and submitted his resignation in May 1862.

Resuming his work in headstones, Fagan expanded his business in April 1877 with the development of Green Hill Cemetery. "Daniel Fagan is making a vigorous effort to get up a cemetery in Luray. He has, in the Eastern suburbs of the town, a beautiful lot which he proposes to divide into squares of sixteen feet, some larger."

By November, Fagan had laid off the walks and drives. Additionally, "a great many of the trees have been set out and the varieties selected are the Cedar, Spruce, and White Pine. The taste displayed so far reflects credit upon its projector, Mr. Daniel Fagan, and when completed it will be an ornament to the town, as well as a great desideratum."

Through the early 1890s, Fagan maintained a strong business that was well received by the community. Many of the most prominent families secured plots at Green Hill. Additionally, beginning in February 1878, Fagan was tasked with reinterring many remains - some from the Old Baptist Graveyard - beginning with his father-in-law, John Simpson.

In 1893, Fagan died and was buried in the cemetery that he had made possible. His wife "Mattie" did not follow until twenty years later in 1913.

Early History of the Page County Finter Family, Part 1
Article of 2/19/2004

From a quick search, the earliest recorded Finters in the area that became known as Page County were Mathias and his son Frederick. According to Richard Branham's 1785 list of the areas that would later encompass the areas now known as Marksville, Leaksville, Stanley, Alma, Honeyville, and Newport, Frederick was living in a household that consisted of two persons while Mathias lived in a household that consisted of five persons. Two other Finter men, perhaps close relatives, were listed in another list as residing near Woodstock (Conrad with 4 family members and Henry with 5). Mathias and Frederick had apparently lived in Lancaster and York County, Pennsylvania before moving to Virginia.

While information on Mathias is particularly hard to come by without in-depth research, Frederick at least left record through his service in the American Revolution. Known to have served in the Continental Line, Frederick was wounded in the elbow at the Battle of Guilford Court House, North Carolina on March 15, 1781. The battle between Continental Army forces under victory by Gen. Nathanael Greene and British forces under Lord Charles Cornwallis resulted in a significant victory in the Southern Campaign and set the stage for Cornwallis' subsequent defeat seven months later at the Siege of Yorktown, Virginia.

A cursory review of Frederick Finter's pension history shows that he, at some point after 1785, removed to Rockbridge County and then later to Orange County where, in 1833 he was still receiving a pension. The pension records frequently reveal two variations of his name (Fender and Finder).

While the family can be traced from Pennsylvania to the Shenandoah Valley, according to one contemporary family historian, several members of the family continued on their migratory route, ending up in the Yadkin River Valley of North Carolina.

At least one of Frederick's children (Jacob) is known to have remained in the area that became Page County. On December 15,

1795, Jacob married Barbara Offenbacker, a daughter of Frederick and Elizabeth Offenbacker.

At least two children (though there were likely more) were known to have come from this marriage. According to her death record in Page County on May 19, 1857, Elizabeth was born at Hawksbill in September 1795. When she died (apparently as a spinster) of dropsy and graval she was living near Columbia Bridge.

A sister, Barbara A. Finter (born ca. 1808) shows no record of having been married and still bore her maiden name in the 1850 Page County census. Interestingly, only a son, Perry, appears in the 1860 census. Children of Barbara A. Finter included Sarah A. Finter (born December 24, 1832 and married to Samuel A. Webster on December 13, 1866); Cullen W. Finter (born May 3, 1837 and married 1) Elizabeth Rowe & 2) Annie C. Nicholson); Charles Hiram Finter (born ca 1844 and married 1) Elizabeth F. Dinges, 2) Rebecca S. Dinges); Perry C. Finter (born April 29, 1846 and married Martha Jane Racer); and Mercy Jane Finter (born October 13, 1848 and married Noah L. Skelton on January 23, 1870).

Early History of the Page County Finter Family, Part 2
Article of 2/26/2004

Though they had not appeared in the 1860 Page County census, it was evident that the Finter family had been overlooked. As the clouds of war gathered around the county, one of the Finter brothers, Cullen, was serving as a major in the 97th Virginia Militia. Though not a regular field unit, the 97th Militia was called up for service on July 13, 1861 and served through September of the same year. After allowing the men ample time to sew the wheat crop, the regiment was again called into service on November 4, 1861. Remaining in active service and operating in the area between Frederick and Hampshire Counties through April 1862, the 97th Regiment was disbanded by order of Gen. Thomas J. "Stonewall" Jackson and the men were encouraged to enlist in regular field units.

Nearly all militia officers, such as Maj. Finter, were relieved of command, though encouraged to enlist in the ranks of other regular field units. With his brother Charles having enlisted in Co. D, 7th Va. Cavalry in April, Cullen enlisted as a private in August. However, while on picket duty near Martinsburg, "Massanutten Rangers" of Co. D, 7th Va. Cavalry along with two other companies came under attack by the 1st New York Cavalry. Several men, including Cullen Finter, were captured and sent off to Atheneum Prison in Wheeling, where they remained for only a few days before being transferred to another prisoner of war camp at Camp Chase, Ohio. Transferred again, within days to Camp Douglas, Illinois, the men were subject to prisoner exchange, but were not exchanged until April 1863.

Cullen rejoined his brother in the ranks, just in time to ride into Pennsylvania. On July 3, 1863, the 7th Virginia, as a part of Gen. "Grumble" Jones's cavalry brigade, was ordered to the little village of Fairfield, where they were to form a line to the right and rear of the main Confederate line at Gettysburg. When within two miles of the village, the Confederates encountered Union cavalry advancing to take the cavalry division's supply wagons. In the fight that ensued, the Federal cavalry laid down a withering fire from their carbines that devastated the 7th Virginia. In the fray, Charles Finter was shot in the back and was captured. With a serious wound to the lung, Charles Finter was sent first to DeCamp Gen. Hospital on David's Island in New York Harbor, and then, by August 24, merited an early exchange on the severity of his wound. Detailed as a Provost Guard in Page County, Charles would not return to the regular service to serve alongside his brother.

Meanwhile, Cullen continued to ride in a number of engagements and could claim the honor of being a part of the 7th when it was designated as a part of the famous "Laurel Brigade" as so named by Gen. Thomas L. Rosser in 1864. Postwar rosters indicate that Perry Finter may have joined Cullen in the field as a member of the "Massanutten Rangers" in late 1864 or early 1865.

While Cullen had served most of the war as a private, his militia title as "major" stayed with him amongst friends and comrades for years after the war and was indicated on his headstone in Green Hill Cemetery. Cullen and his brother Perry were among the over 200 Page County Confederates who, in September 1881, attended a reunion with the Captain Colwell Post No. 201, G.A.R. from Carlisle, Pa. which had, just two months before, come to Luray at the invitation of the Page Confederates. Today, descendants of both Cullen and Perry continue to reside in Page County.

The Forrer Family –
From Clockmakers to Iron Magnates and Socialites
Article of 1/16/2003

Most of those who live in Page County, if they know the background of the Forrer family in the county, remember them more for their reign as the "iron magnates" and relation to Furnaces No. 1 & 2 and Catherine's Furnace. However, the focus of a family book, *Christian Forrer, Clockmaker* written in 1939 by Frank Bruen focuses first on the clockmaker as progenitor of the Forrer line in America.

The son of Daniel and Anna Engel Fuhrer (both died in Mett, Switzerland in the 1740s), Christian Forrer was known as a traditional Swiss Mennonite clockmaker. It is not known for certain if the art was acquired through the family or as work as an apprentice. Christian practiced the fine art, but, to date, only five tall or grandfather clocks were known to be made by him. Christian Forrer's artful work as a maker of clock works is highly respected and the handful of known works highly sought after. While locating his works today is an extreme rarity, one of Forrer's works is illustrated in *Clockmakers of Lancaster County And Their Clocks, 1750-1850*. Another is now with the Levy Gallery in New York. Made primarily of cherry and including secondary wood from pine and poplar, the Queen Anne Tall Clock, was built ca. 1755 in Lampeter, Pennsylvania.

Christian married Elizabeth Kendrick, a daughter of Heinrich and Maria Wolfe Kendig, before 1765. The Kendig/Kundig line actually can be traced to the mid 1500s in Auslikon, Pfafficon, Switzerland.

Christian and Elizabeth eventually settled near Luray, along with at least one other Kendrick family member. Samuel, a son of Christian and Elizabeth and experienced iron man of Pennsylvania, brought forth the age of iron to the Forrer family in Page County. His sons, Henry and Daniel continued the tradition. However, while the Forrer family was fairly well occupied with the Shenandoah Iron Works, Daniel was also busy elsewhere with an extension of the "empire" into Augusta County with the founding of the Mossy Creek Iron Works as early as the late 1840s.

Interestingly, there is a most fascinating social tie that was initiated as a sidebar to the Forrer ironworks "empire." With the introduction of New Yorker Jedediah Hotchkiss to Henry Forrer in Luray, Henry, in turn, introduced Jedediah (Jed) to his brother Daniel at Mossy Creek. In need of a scholar to tutor his children, Daniel found what he was looking for in Jed. By 1852, the tutorship turned much larger with the development of the Mossy Creek Academy. Despite it being in Augusta County, the knowledge of the academy was spread well among Luray social elite, eventually leading to several children of the well-to-do Luray citizens, such as the Jordans and Lionbergers, to attendance of Hotchkiss' school.

Apart from the handful of descendants who remain in the area (less the Forrer surname now), a few entries in local history books and pamphlets, and the graves of Forrer family members at Evergreen, Green Hill and the Forrer-Kendrick Cemeteries, little evidence remains today of the family that was busy in social circles in Luray and Page and was once vital to one of Page County's most thriving industries of years gone by.

The Gibbons Family in Page County, Part 1
Article of 9/25/2003

Though I take on the subject of the Gibbons Family in this article, I would certainly say that one man would have tackled the subject with much greater insight than I. Years ago, when I was first embarking on my own in-depth research efforts into the history of Page County, I met a man full of knowledge who was writing a book about the Gibbons family. Mr. Alfred M. Gibbons knew virtual store loads of information about the family . . . so much that it was his intent to write a book on them and the way the family's history intertwined with that of Page in the early 19th century. I do not know what happened to Mr. Gibbons as we lost touch in the early 90s, but I wish to dedicate this article to him. I treasure the memories of our meetings and discussions about the Gibbons family.

From a trace on the web and a sifting through a little known local history, the immigrant progenitor of this particular Gibbons family was Abel Gibbons. Born in Wales ca. 1720, Abel married twice. Though the name of Abel's first wife name appears to be lost to time, Abel's first two children were John & Isaac Gibbons. Isaac later becomes the family link into the Shenandoah Valley.

From Isaac, the lines of the Shenandoah Valley Gibbons families become a little clearer. Isaac was born on March 13, 1757 and eventually served in the American Revolution as a member of the Pennsylvania Dragoons, according to a list of pensioners in Shenandoah County under the Act of March 18, 1818. Following his time in the war, on December 28, 1782, he married Mary Gangwer, the daughter of John George Gangwer and Magdalena Gleifer. The first of Isaac and Mary's children were born in Shamokin Valley, Pennsylvania from between 1784 through 1791. However, shortly thereafter, the family had made their way into the Shenandoah Valley, settling at Woodstock. The last (and eleventh!) child, Samuel, was born on June 17, 1806.

Nevertheless, according to Alfred M. Gibbon's portion of *Shenandoah: A History of Our Town and It's People*, "'Sam' had known many hardships as a boy," laboring in his father's fields "from dusk to dawn." By the age of 12, Samuel was "bound out" to his eldest brother John as an apprentice carpenter, while helping build John's "Locust Dale" manor house beside the river near McGaheysville. Having "bought" his time out by erecting a "fine retirement home for Capt. Henry Miller, Jr., near Elk Run Creek (Elkton), and having been granted the hand of Christina Miller, Samuel set out to start a life of his own.

By 1830, following the birth of their first daughter near McGaheysville, the Samuel Gibbons Family moved to a "log dwelling" along the South Fork near where the bridge crosses near the present day town of Shenandoah. In short order, with the assistance of his father-in-law, Samuel purchased two adjoining tracts totaling some 1,100 acres.

Without going into great detail and desiring to remain focused on examining the lesser-known portion of the family history, in time, this purchase would lead to the famous Forrer, Gibbons & Forrer partnership that was the beginning of the Shenandoah Iron Works; a subject that has been well-documented in a few publications about Page County.

Beyond the future iron ore endeavor, Samuel would also be involved in political circles in the formation of Page County and was nominated by the justices of the newly formed county to occupy a "seat on the bench beside them" and was also appointed the 28th magistrate as well as overseer of the public road from the old county line to the new line . . . all of this in addition to his ongoing trade as a carpenter!

The Gibbons Family in Page County, Part 2 Article of 10/9/2003

Between their time in residence at Shenandoah Iron Works (1830-1844) and at Willow Grove Farm (1844-1860), the Gibbons family had six children. While residing at Willow Grove, as new members of the family were growing up on the farm, Samuel Gibbon's mother, Mary Gangwer Gibbons died in 1851 and was the first family member to be laid to rest in the family plot on the hill just above the mill. By August 1859, one of the Gibbons children, 24 year-old Samuel Peyton Gibbons became a second family member to be laid to rest in the cemetery near Luray.

Despite the family deaths, the Samuel Gibbons family continued to make strides for the better. Ultimately, the wealth gained by Samuel Gibbons in selling his interests in the iron works to the Forrer family is evident as he was able to send three of his sons to the Virginia Military Institute.

The first son, Simeon Beauford Gibbons (born 5/25/1833) left Willow Grove to matriculate at VMI in 1848 along with Page County natives Hiram Jackson Strickler and William Overall Yager. Strickler only attended for two years, however, both Yager and Gibbons continued until graduation in 1852 with a ranking of 5th and 7th of 24 respectively. Simeon returned briefly to Page County and taught school briefly near Hudson's just across from Willow Grove. Later moving to Harrisonburg, Simeon became a merchant and married Fannie Shacklett in 1855 who died less than a year later.

As the 1850s drew to a close, the Gibbons family prepared for yet another move and sold the Willow Grove Farm in 1860. The youngest son, Alfred Ringold Gibbons (born 8/6/1846), recalled that the family moved to Rome, Georgia by the fall of 1860. This was not long after a second son, William Stephens Gibbons (born 7/27/1842), entered VMI in July.

With the outbreak of the Civil War, the family was caught with the family apart in two states. In Virginia, "Sim" was made colonel of the 10th Virginia Infantry while brother William was detailed as a drillmaster in Richmond and Harpers Ferry, drilling both Co. K, 10th Va. Infantry (from Page) and Co. K, 1st Tennessee Infantry. Meanwhile in Georgia, John Selden Gibbons (born 9/11/1840) enlisted with Co. A, 8th Georgia Infantry (The Rome Guards).

Ultimately, John would be the first of the sons to fall in the war, not dying in battle, but of typhoid in Centerville, Virginia on July 21, 1861. He would be the last Gibbons buried in the plot near Willow Grove. Less than 10 months later, Col. "Sim" Gibbons was mortally wounded while leading his regiment in battle at McDowell, Virginia. His brother William, serving as his brother's orderly, reached the colonel just after he had died. Simeon was laid to rest next to his beloved wife in Woodbine Cemetery in Harrisonburg.

Ultimately, the war would not claim anymore in combat, but the adventures of the two remaining brothers are worthy of note. After Simeon's death, Alfred matriculated at Georgia Military Institute in Marietta and was soon after detailed to help build fortifications around Atlanta and to guard POWs. Meanwhile, William enlisted with the Page Volunteers of Co. K, 10th Va. Inf. However, due to health, was discharged in January 1863.

The Gibbons Family in Page County, Part 3 Article of 10/16/2003

In August 1863, Alfred R. Gibbons left the Georgia Military Institute and matriculated at VMI, the third and last son to do so. Alfred recalled that while at VMI "from the 1st of September up to the middle of December, the Corps of Cadets was ordered out to repel Federal raids three or four times and were out from ten days to two weeks. The last and longest time was our roughest, as while we were in the mountains we had a hard rain that turned to snow, with freezing weather, and as we had to wade many of the streams, our pants would be frozen stiff. We had not tents, only blankets, to protect us from the rain and snow. While we did no fighting we learned about the hardships of soldier life. The last of December, I resigned from the Institute and went back to Georgia and joined the regular army" (Co. G, 1st Georgia Cavalry).

While Alfred began his service in the field on March 6, 1864, by May 1, 1864, William's health had returned and he also entered the service but with Co. C, 39th Battalion Virginia Cavalry, rejoining several old friends from Page County. While theaters apart in the war, both were captured later that summer. William at Hedgesville, near Martinsburg, on June 28 and Alfred near Atlanta on July 21.

Ultimately, the Federals tried three times to convict William of spying and in the end he "narrowly escaped death." Without the conviction they sought, William was sent to Camp Chase, Ohio where he was held until exchanged in March 1865.

Alfred's exploits after his capture are well documented in his thirty-one page *Recollections of An Old Confederate Soldier*. Jumping from the POW train that was transporting him to Camp Chase, he tried to make his way South again. However, while moving through Illinois, he stole some clothes and a horse and was caught. Facing a penitentiary offence, he chose to go to jail instead of being returned as a Confederate POW, knowing he would receive significantly better treatment in the Illinois Pen. After the close of the war, with the help of his father, Alfred secured a pardon from the governor and was released in September 1865.

Though the war had ended, in January 1866, William again faced issues that once again put him in dire circumstances concerning the former war. Arrested by U.S. authorities, he, along with four other men were taken to Atlanta and kept in confinement for three weeks. The reason behind the arrest evolved around the fact that a Confederate flag was owned by his family and had been used in a tableau in which the other four took part. Fortunately, William was let go and returned to civilian life. Gibbons served as a druggist from 1865-1872 before he moved his farm near Rome, Georgia. In 1877 he married Ella J. Pitner and had a family of at least six children. William died in April 1931.

Alfred moved to Shelbina, Missouri in 1867, married first in 1869 (eight children) and again in 1883 (four children). The youngest son of the second marriage, Boone, was born in 1892 and was the father of the same Alfred M. Gibbons who, in the 1980s, wrote the Samuel Gibbons family story for the book *Shenandoah, A History of Our Town and Its People.*

Little is known about the only sister. Louisa Urmanilla Gibbons was born September 29, 1830 and married Rome, Georgia native James H. Presley in 1870. At least one child was born to the couple.

The Ham Family in Page County
Article of 5/6/2004

While no clear record of their entry into Page County can be found at present, at least two children of Joseph H. Ham and Anne Grace Smoot entered Page County around the 1830s.

Born in 1807, Elijah Ham married Sarah Armentrout in 1833. At least nine children were born to this union. As Elijah and his wife appear to have made their home near or just across the Page-Rockingham County line somewhere between Shenandoah Iron Works and Conrad's Store (now Elkton), the majority of their descendants can be found in the records of Rockingham County.

Elijah's sister, Sarah Ann Ham, married William Dorraugh in Page County in 1837. From this union also came at least nine children. William and Sarah lived in the vicinity of Somerville, near what is now known as Grove Hill in Page County, and, as it turns out, the majority of children from this line left heirs in Page County among the Dofflemoyer, Emerson, Milton and other families in the area.

But from whence did the Ham family originate?

There are two conflicting studies about the origins of the Ham family in Virginia or at least the Culpeper County Ham line from whom the Page County Ham family descended. One trace shows that the family is descended from a Jerome Ham. Born in Bristol, Somersetshire, England around 1577, Jerome was married to Sibilla Cainhoe, the daughter of Rev. William Caynehoe (who died in York County, Virginia in 1644). Jerome served as Justice of the Peace, High Sheriff and Burgess for York County, Virginia.

Another possibility would tie the family to one Joseph Ham who emigrated, at age 16, from England to Elizabeth City, Virginia aboard the *Warwick* in 1621 as the indentured servant of Lieutenant Albiano Lupo. After serving his seven years, Joseph Ham did well for himself and was at one point listed as having land in Charles River County (now York County). His will, dated March 1637/38 listed him as having 2,000 pounds of tobacco and 20 young goats.

While the specific connections cannot yet be established, it appears that Joseph H. Ham, the man from whom we began this story, was the son of Samuel Ham and Milly Sutting of Spotsylvania County. Born ca. 1722, Samuel was also the son of yet another Samuel (born ca. 1700) who may have been either the son to Jerome Ham who was the son of the original Jerome Ham or Joseph Ham.

Recently a detailed history of the Ham family has been written and may shed a great deal of light onto the otherwise uncertain linkages in the family. Titled *A Short History of the Ham Surname in Virginia & North Carolina*, the three-volume work includes nearly 1,300 pages including 100 pages of bibliographic references and nearly 200 pages of indices. Based upon original records, manuscripts and books, these volumes are arranged chronologically, fully indexed by surname, places, with illustrations, full bibliographies, and citations to sources. Printed in December 2003, the book is available from Gateway Press, Inc., Baltimore, Maryland.

The Harris Family in Page County
Article of 8/26/2004

The name William Alexander Harris should be no stranger to the annals of Page County history. Though being born in 1805 in Fauquier County, William Harris, Sr. moved to Page County (then Shenandoah County) by the 1820's as a young lawyer and was first noted for an article that he wrote about the Luray Cave in the 1825 *Shenandoah Herald*. Harris may have been one of the fifteen original men to have thoroughly explored the cave that year. A delegate to the Virginia House in 1830, Harris could be considered one of the founders of Page County, having secured the passage of the bill dividing Shenandoah and Page County. As the first Clerk of the Court beginning May 23, 1831, and attorney for the Commonwealth, Harris was also appointed as one of the commissioners to oversee the construction of the county offices. In September, 1837, the elder Harris continued in his multi-faceted roles and was responsible for donations for the opening of a road through Milam's Gap. In 1840, Harris held the distinguished position as Presidential elector on the Martin Van Buren and Johnson ticket. The following year he was forced to resign as Clerk of the Court for his new post in the U.S. Congress (1841-1843). In his resignation Harris wrote, ". . . I may be permitted to express my grateful sense of the kindness and friendly courtesy which have at all times been extended to me by every member of the Court." Before his retiring to private life the elder Harris held a host of other positions including editor of *The Speculator* and *The Constitution*, Charge de affairs to the Argentine Republic, editorship of the D.C. paper *Washington Union*, and printer to the U.S. Senate from 1857 to 1859. Harris eventually settled permanently in Pike County, Missouri during the Civil War and died in 1864.

William Harris, Jr. had been born in Loudoun County while the elder Harris was a member of Congress from Virginia. First educated at Columbian College (now George Washington University), William Harris, Jr. had matriculated as part of the third or sophomore class at VMI on January 16, 1860. Official records reveal that he matriculated from Page County, though he actually had done so from Pike County, Missouri. In a class composed of future notables such as future commanding officer of the Stuart Horse Artillery, Roger Preston Chew, Harris fared well in class standing, graduating early in December, 1861 as 7 of 35. After his brief stint as drillmaster with Page County's Dixie Artillery, Harris was assigned to duty with Col. William N. Pendleton and, in the same month (Nov. 1861) transferred as assistant adjutant general on the staff of General Cadmus Wilcox. Promoted to captain in January 1862, Harris resigned from Wilcox's staff in July 1862 and was assigned as a lieutenant and acting ordinance officer in Gen. Daniel Harvey Hill's division. Promoted to the temporary rank of captain in the spring of 1863, Harris was yet reassigned and named Chief of Ordinance of Gen. Robert E. Rodes' division. Following the loss at Gettysburg, Harris deserted from the army feeling that further effort was futile. However, some records reveal that he may have had other reasons for leaving the army in that he was denied a transfer to Major Harry W. Gilmor's cavalry battalion.

In 1865 Harris and his Page County native bride, Mary Lionberger did not return to Page to settle. Instead, Harris found his fortune in Kansas as a civil engineer for the Union Pacific Railroad. Following in his father's footsteps, Harris eventually sought a life in politics, first as a member of the Populist party and later as a democrat (1896), becoming a U.S. Congressman from Kansas (1893-1895), a member of the Kansas State Senate (1896), a U.S. senator from Kansas (1897-1903), and an unsuccessful candidate for the governorship of Kansas in 1906. It is said that Harris was "the only Confederate ever elected to any office of importance in Kansas." Harris was extremely popular in the agriculture circles for his raising shorthorn cattle. Retiring from political life, Harris later became the vice president of the Denver, Laramie & Northwestern Railroad. He died in Chicago while serving in that role in 1909. Harris' widow later served as a delegate to the 1916 Democratic National Convention.

Huffman Family Origins
Article of 8/12/2004

According to the 1860 census there were no less than ten heads of family with the name of Huffman in Page County at that time. Of all of those listed, most can easily be traced to ancestors born in the 1760s or 1770s – Daniel, born in 1764; Frederick, born in 1768, Christian, born in 1773; and Abraham. While definite parental ties for Christian and Frederick cannot be clearly established, Abraham and Daniel were sons of George Huffman.

Born in 1745, George was a son (there were 10 sons and 4 daughters in all) of John Henry Huffman of the 1714 Germanna Colony. John Henry Huffman (otherwise known as Johannes Heinrich Hoffman) was born in 1692 in Siegen, Nassau-Siegen, Germany, a son of Johannes (1663 – 1731) and Gertrud Hoffman. According to an issue (April, 1963) of the *Germanna Record* his family lived in Eisern, in the southern part of the principality. "Eisern was included in the Catholic part of Nassau-Siegen, though the Hoffman family were Protestants." Johannes' (1663) father was Tillmann Hoffman who was a "Fuhrmann" or carrier – which basically equates to having been an exporter of iron goods – from Nassau-Siegen to other parts of Germany. After exporting iron goods, Tillmann would return bringing imports with him. According to the same issue of the *Germanna Record*, Tillmann, his father and grandfather "all lived in Eisern, were all admitted smelterers to the Guild of Smelterers and Hammersmiths at various times (showing that they were part owners of some smelter or ironworks, probably at Eisern ironworks). Tillmann was also an associate justice of the district court, the Haingericht.

While I have written before about the colony at Germanna and how several of Page County's Germanic families came lay claim to ancestry from that colony, I have yet to write about the village of Germantown, where many of the Germanna colonists relocated after the original colony had folded. Johannes (1692) Hoffman was among the eleven families that moved to Germantown around 1719, and married on November 7, 1721 to Anna Catherine Haeger (born in Siegen, May 15, 1702). Anna was a daughter of Rev. Henry Haeger, the pastor of the 1714 colony, and his wife Katherine Friesenhagen, daughter of Jacob Friesenhagen, Mayor of

Freudenberg. Rev. Henry Haeger was a son of Henry Haeger of Antzhausen and his second wife Guda. Johannes and Anna had at least three children before Anna died. Sometime following Anna's death, Johannes remarried and the union produced at least twelve children, including George.

Within eight years of his first marriage, Johannes Hoffman and his family moved again in 1729 to the Robinson River section near the Germanna Colony of 1717, and died there in 1772, in what was then Culpeper County/now Madison County.

Exactly when the Huffman family transitioned to the area now known as Page County is uncertain without a dedicated search of deed books. However, George Huffman, son of Johannes, was apparently among the first. According to James Huffman's *Ups and Downs of a Confederate Soldier*, James recalled, in later years, the "Grape Vine Meeting House on the riverside just below the new steel bridge that now spans the Shenandoah at Alma" and that his great grandfather, George Huffman, grandfather, Daniel Huffman, grandmother Catherine Huffman, and dear little brother Willie, about ten months old" who were all buried in "a little graveyard nearby." Regretfully, at a quick glance of the cemetery records of Page County, none of these names can be found among the headstones recorded in the latter part of the 20th century.

If there is a connection between all of the Huffman families of Page County, it is not easily revealed in identifying the burial sites of the earlier mention progenitors of the different lines – Daniel, Frederick, Christian and Abraham. While the locations of Daniel (and his wife Margaret Bumgardner) and Abraham Huffman's (and his wife/wives Mary Comer or Elizabeth Dinkle) graves remain unknown; Christian and his wife Christina Gochenour Huffman are buried in the Henry Huffman cemetery in Luray; and Frederick Huffman (his wife was Susannah Beidler) is buried in the Huffman/Brubaker Cemetery in Stanley.

The Man Behind the Mansion Inn: A Glimpse at the Life of Gabriel Jordan, Sr., Part 1

Article of 6/10/2004

At various times over the past few years, this column has included stories about the former Mansion Inn and several children of Gabriel and Elizabeth Ann Siebert Jordan, including Thomas Jordan, Macon Jordan, Francis H. "Frank" Jordan (and his wife Cornelia), and there has even been a quick write-up about Gabriel Jordan, Jr. But what about the life of Gabriel Jordan, Sr.?

Born ca. 1793 to Thomas Jordan, Gabriel Jordan has somewhat of a difficult ancestry to trace. According to a website about Walter Coles of Pittsylvania County (he married Gabriel's daughter, Lavinia Catherine Jordan in 1862), Gabriel was of English ancestry and his father, "Thomas Jordan, fought in the revolution, associated with the Marquis De Lafayette." Apparently, because of this association with the famous Frenchman, Luray just narrowly missed notoriety as having been one of the many different towns and cities visited in the 1820s by Lafayette. In a letter written in 1824 to Gabriel "the Marquis De Lafayette regrets his inability to visit him, 'the worthy son of my gallant old Comrade in arms, Thomas Jordan.'"

Regretfully, there is a missing link between Gabriel's father, Thomas, and the earlier line of Jordans in Virginia. While there appears to be an obvious link in the mid-1800s between the Page County Jordans and a number of families in and around Lynchburg and also Campbell, Pittyslvania and Halifax Counties, little else is of help in quickly identifying how and when a branch of the Jordan family made their way to what we know as Page County today. According to the Works Progress Administration records of Page County and an interview made with one of Gabriel Jordan's descendants in the 1930s, Gabriel was believed to have been a descendant (perhaps great grandson) of Thomas Jordan and Mary Brasseur. If this is the case, this particular Thomas Jordan (born ca. 1634 in Nansemond County, Va.) was one of Virginia's earliest Quakers, and, subsequently, his father, also named Thomas, was connected to Virginia's Jamestown Colony.

Nevertheless, it is still unclear as to when Gabriel settled in the Shenandoah Valley. In October 1818, Gabriel made his first appearance in area records when he married Betsy Ann Siebert (daughter of Francis Siebert, born ca. 1777) in Woodstock, Shenandoah County. The couple's first child, Thomas Jordan, was born in the Luray Valley on September 30, 1819. By January 1829, Gabriel had been appointed postmaster of Luray. This was, no doubt, amidst the time when Gabriel Jordan's wealth was rapidly growing from his successful endeavors as a merchant with stores in both Luray and Honeyville.

Soon after the establishment of Page County in 1831, Jordan continued to hold his place as one of the most prominent men of the area and began to share the wealth gained by him through his successful mercantile business. As one of the men figuring regularly in the county court dealings, Jordan permitted one of his houses to be outfitted as a county jail in the June 28, 1831 session of county court. He was also appointed as one of a small number of men to select plans for the jail. A month later, on July 28, 1831, court was actually held in the Jordan Family home, at which time Jordan and his wife deeded property to the county for the construction of a county courthouse; that particular lot having been originally bought by Jordan from the Marye family.

While Jordan was most generous in the early history of the creation of some of the county's earliest public buildings, he also figured prominently in his religious beliefs and, on July 4, 1833, he and his wife conveyed property to the Trustees of the Methodist Episcopal Church so that a house of worship could be constructed, "adjoining the graveyard lot." The donation is interesting as Gabriel's wife, Bettie, was known by her obituary to have been Old School Baptist since the age of 13. Likewise, it is believed that Gabriel may have also been of the Baptist faith.

The Man Behind the Mansion Inn: A Glimpse at the Life of Gabriel Jordan, Sr., Part 2 Article of 6/17/2004

Through his mercantile business and his donation of lands for public use, Gabriel Jordan figured prominently as a respectable citizen of Page County through the mid-1800s. Jordan also figured prominently in the lives of local children. Not only was he the guardian of Hiram Strickler (as chosen by Hiram in court on April 27, 1846), who had been left an orphan after the death of his father, Abraham (Daniel Forrer, another prominent businessman of Page was appointed the guardian of Rebecca Strickler, Hiram's sister), Gabriel also took in fifteen year-old George Morgan Jones in the late 1830s, not long after the death of his father, Wharton Jones. With the permission of his mother (Nancy Wood Jones), George Morgan Jones, left "Pleasant View on Jeremy's Run for Luray in 1839 to accept employment as clerk in a general store owned by Gabriel Jordan. Having left school at the age of fifteen to start out on his career as a merchant, George apparently found his true vocation. According to a website about George, "Even though he was only a boy, he made his impressions upon his employer and his customers by his careful attention to business, and his courtesy and consideration for the rights of the buyer. George Jones spent six years with Mr. Jordan in Luray, developing his business talents in this excellent school." Though the "close confinement and irregular hours finally proved too much . . . at age twenty-one he encountered his first serious obstacle, ill health, which compelled him to resign his position." Though he left the Page Valley and eventually settled in Lynchburg, the lessons of his youth, under the guidance of Gabriel Jordan, figured heavily in his future success as a businessman in Lynchburg. Jones was later not only known as the head of the mercantile firm known as Jones, Watts & Company, but also as president of the National Exchange Bank, president of the Cotton Manufacturing Company and first president of the Lynchburg Board of Trade.

Continuing his longstanding support of community projects, by February 1849, Gabriel Jordan had expanded his interests and was listed at that time as one of the trustees of the Shenandale College at

New Market. Though the college was short-lived, a primary focus of study at the institution was on agriculture.

According to one of the aforementioned websites, Gabriel Jordan was ever the " "patriotic citizen" throughout the mid-1800s, "devoting his life to the improvement of the section of the country in which he lived; a man of many affairs." By the outbreak of the American Civil War, Jordan "had accumulated considerable wealth" (listed in the 1860 census as being a "gentleman" with over $85,400 in real estate) and played prominently in the fundraising efforts in Page County to appropriate uniform and equipment for volunteer companies that would be formed in the county. A member of the committee on issuing county bonds for the support of county volunteer units, Jordan also personally took on the task of "fitting out a cavalry company (the Massanutten Rangers; also known as Co. D, 7th Virginia Cavalry) at his own expense." Two of his sons initially served as officers in the unit – Macon Jordan as its first captain.

Gabriel Jordan died while visiting Lynchburg in January 1862. According to a letter of the time, he was to be brought home to Luray for burial. According to one source, he is supposedly buried in the mausoleum in the rear of the Baptist parsonage in Luray. However, as there are no markings on the mausoleum to indicate that Gabriel is buried there, this cannot be confirmed. Gabriel's wife, Betsy Ann Siebert Jordan, died on October 4, 1883 at the home of her daughter, Bettie Hackley, in Washington, Rappahannock County.

While this column has featured Gabriel and Betsy Siebert Jordan's sons in the past (Thomas, Francis H., Macon and Gabriel Jr.), the four daughters, Ann (born ca. 1825), Gabriella (b. ca. 1831), Lavinia Catherine (born in 1833 and mentioned in last week's article) and Bettie Ellen were all married to men from throughout Virginia, not from Page County. Ann and Gabriella married a set of Meem brothers from Shenandoah County (Andrew Russell Meem and Gilbert S. Meem, respectfully). Lavinia married Walter Coles of Pittsylvania County in 1862 and Bettie Ellen married W.B. Hackley of Culpeper County in 1875.

Carl Sebastian Keyser:
The Forerunner of the Page County Keysers
Article 11/27/2003

There is a considerable amount of research moving forward recently that leads back to the roots of the Page County Keyser families. One of the groundbreaking findings takes us to one Carl Sebastian Kayser. Previously, Keyser researchers have known that Carl Keyser, Sr. was the progenitor of the line in Page County, but some recently discovered information has been proven earlier information either incorrect or slightly off. Born about 1 a.m. on January 16, 1725 (not 1702 as previously believed), in Mockmuhl (not Wurttemberg as previously believed), Germany, Carl was the son of Andreas and Catherina Kayser. Andreas was, by trade, a butcher, and was the son of Johann Casper Keyser, also a butcher in Mockmuhl. Andreas' wife (actually his second wife), Anna Catherina, was the daughter of Johannes Ruffnacher, a farmer in Brettach. While it is yet unclear when Andreas died, Catherina (born approximately 23 April 1697) died on 24 August 1755 in Mockmuhl.

Carl Sebastian Kayser immigrated, while a servant to one Johan Jacob Eicholtz (a butcher and future innkeeper), to America as early as September 1749. Records supporting the early date of immigration (he was previously believed to have immigrated in either 1751 or 1752 according to a few references) include two records of Holy Communion at the Evangelical Lutheran Church of the Holy Trinity Church in Lancaster, Pa. where he actually settled initially. Apparently, by 1751 Karl married Mary Shelley. Within a year, the first child, Charles, Jr., was born to the new couple.

A butcher by trade, Karl (Carl) was soon called into the service of the British army in the colonies. Benjamin Franklin's autobiography states that Franklin was asked by General Edward Braddock to secure, for his army, more wagons to haul supplies for the march to Ft. Duquesne. One of the places which he solicited such wagons was in Lancaster County, supporting the belief that Keyser had, by 1755, been with Braddock, perhaps as a part of the army's quartermaster department (as a butcher). In the spring of 1755, Braddock's army (approximately 2,400 strong) departed Alexandria, Virginia for the attack on Ft. Duquesne. Certainly, it would have been great to hear family stories passed down through the Keyser family about the march to Ft. Duquesne, but little is known except through the history books that Braddock was subsequently defeated on July 9 and ultimately died from wounds sustained in the fight.

From this point there is a gap in understanding what happened in Carl's life. However, by 6 April 1765, Carl appears to have purchased land along the South Fork of the Shenandoah in the part of Frederick County that would (more than 65 years later) become Page County.

Before Carl died in 1778, he and his wife would have several children, including Charles (Carl, Jr.), John, Andre, Joseph, David, Michael, Anna, Mary, Esther and Kate. Note many of the names, including that of Andrew, mirrored family names, such as Andreas.

The Kite Family of Page County, Part 1 Article of 9/19/2002

For sometime, I've been leery of taking this family on as a subject as it is such a large family. Even though I too have direct Kite ancestry, the task is immense. Ultimately, I have found that some early resources published in the early 20th century are misleading, and, originally led me in the wrong direction several years ago in tracing the family tree. One source even leads one to believe that the family may have been of English origin, which is actually more than likely, incorrect. Many of the works being developed in contemporary times seem to be more careful and accurate, utilizing several of the resources that were unavailable to many of the earlier researchers.

The earliest known name in the lineage takes the Kite family back to the middle 1600s with a Philip Wendle Kite. A son, John Windle Kite or Windlekite/Windlekeit, can more or less be seen as the progenitor of the family in the Page Valley. Born about 1698, John married Eve Elizabeth Jones in Augusta County around 1720. Little is known of John except that in 1747 he was fined for swearing in court. John died in Augusta County on November 26, 1751. Eve is a little more elusive and doesn't give a clear trail.

In my own research, I have found that John and Eve had at least four sons, George, John, Philip and William Windle Kite. William Windle Kite is the link that I have found to be the source for Page County Kites. William was probably born around 1732 in what appears to be Augusta County, though some sources allude to his having come from Radnor, Pennsylvania. He married Catherine Mifford (of Orange County) in Rockingham County around 1759. William died in 1805 in Rockingham County and Catherine died about 1843.

With the children of William and Catherine, a clearer picture begins to unfold. Among the children were Adam, William, Reuben, Martin, Benjamin, Elizabeth, and John. Most of the children, excepting Martin, seem to have remained in the area known today as Rockingham County. Some of William Kites heirs, as a matter of fact, have the tie with the famous Miller-Kite House in Elkton.

Martin Kite, as indicated, continues the line of "succession" in Page County. Born in Augusta County around 1776, he married Catherine Kiser (or, as other records indicate, he could have married Elizabeth Koiner, daughter of George Adam & Barbara Smith Koiner), daughter of Michael and Anna Maria Eppart Kiser in 1788 in Rockingham County. Martin died in 1823 and Catherine followed sometime after between 1823 and 1838. Among the children of Martin and Catherine/Elizabeth? were Elizabeth, George, Jacob C., Mary, John, James Stephen, and David B. Kite; all born between 1790 and 1806.

There are several more commonly known names that unfold in Page County beginning with the bloodline from Martin and Catherine/Elizabeth and will be detailed in a small way in the next article.

The Kite Family of Page County, Part 2 Article of 10/3/2002

While several Kite family members merit inclusion in the history of Page County, part 1 of this overview left us with the children of Martin (born ca. 1766) and his wife. Of the seven children from this marriage, marriages were made into the Armentrout, Foltz, Long, Slagel, Henkle, Conrad, and Kauffman family lines.

The 1816 marriage between Mary Kite and Ambrose Henkle/Henkel (his second marriage) is a rather interesting one, showing the dynamics of cultural interaction with Page County families with those from across the Massanutten at New Market. Ambrose Henkel was the son of Paul and Catherine Hoke Henkel. The association may actually bring some merit in the presumption that the Kite family name may have originally been Wendlekeit or something similar of German origin. Indeed, the famous German publishing company known as the Henkel Press was, in fact, started by Mary Kite's husband. Additionally, the Henkel Press also produced the first German newspaper printed below the Mason-Dixon line and was known as *The Virginia and New Market Popular Instructor and Weekly News*. Ambrose actually sold the press to his brother Solomon in 1816 or 1817 in order to dedicate time to becoming a Lutheran minister. Ambrose was ordained in either 1823 or 1824. Mary Kite Henkel died in 1826.

Likewise, James Stephen Kite's marriage to Margaret Conrad (of the same family that bestowed the name to the town of Conrad's Store, now known as Elkton) also exhibits the wide area of affiliations in which the Kite family engaged.

A particularly famous individual from Page County history was Noah Kite, actually a nephew of Martin Kite and the son of Benjamin Kite. Noah was best known for his operations at Columbia Mills, near Alma. As many know, Noah, his wife Isabella, and children Edward Lee Kite, Ashby Jackson Kite, Endora Angeline Kite and Eleanor Catherine Kite Nauman were all killed in the terrible flood on September 29, 1870.

While the story was tragic for all involved, the story of Eleanor was particularly sad. Eleanor had married Hiram G. Nauman only seven months before. Hiram's father, Reuben, owned the large brick mercantile store at the intersection of the old Blue Ridge/New Market to Gordonsville Turnpike & the Luray to Staunton Turnpike at Honeyville, not far from Noah Kite's mill. According to the Jacob Seekford story, Eleanor was also pregnant with the newlyweds first child at the time of the flood. Seekford wrote "Mr. Nauman had not yet taken his wife from home and if Honey Run could have been crossed the night of the flood Mr. Nauman would have been at the Kite home instead of being at the home of his father at Honeyville."

A monument, dedicated in 1938, stands today near the site of the Noah Kite Home.

The Pence Family in Page County
Article of 5/13/2004

As with a vast number of families to eventually settle in Page County, the Pence or Bentz Family had roots to Germany – specifically the area near Iggelheim, Pfalz, Bayern, Germany. In all likelihood, Johann George Bentz was the earliest known link to the line of Pence families that are in Page County today. Married to Anna Barbara Bullinger (daughter of Jacob & Anna Katherine Webber Bullinger), Bentz/Pence immigrated to America in 1749 aboard the *Phoenix* and arriving in Philadelphia. Of the eight known children of this couple, four were known to have settled in the Shenandoah Valley.

However, though at least four sons were known to have settled in the Shenandoah Valley (some even around Marksville near the Little Hawksbill Creek), married and had children, by the early 1810s, the bulk of the Pence family moved at various times to counties in Ohio, Kentucky, Missouri and Illinois.

So, where did the modern line of Page County Pence family members come from? Though he later immigrated to Champaign County, Ohio, one of Johann George Pence's sons, Henry, had a son (by marriage with Mary Magdalene Blimly) named George. Born in 1766 in Frederick County, George married Mary Mauck (daughter of Daniel Mauck and Barbara Harnsberger). One of the children to come from this union was Peter Pence, born around 1800.

Apparently, Peter remained in the area that later became known as Page County. Peter married Sophia Aleshire in 1823 and settled just east of Alma along Stoney Run.

As the sole remainder of the early Bentz/Pence family in Page County, by the time of the Civil War, the family would endure events peculiar to some families of the area. While several sons "wore the gray," one son, Abraham, had relocated to Iowa and served in the Union army. While it is likely that any of the brothers ever saw the brother in blue across a field of battle, the Confederate Pence sons - Isaac Newton Pence and Wesley F. Pence – served in both the Dixie and Purcell Artillery. Isaac was said to have been killed at Petersburg in 1865 but postwar ledgers for the Purcell Artillery indicate that he may have died in a military hospital of disease. Wesley was captured about the time of Gettysburg and spent the balance of the war in Ft. Delaware as a POW, being release on May 8, 1865. Yet another brother, William, served in Co. H, 33rd Va. Inf. and was an unfortunate one among a group pf Page County men from the same unit who deserted and were given the chance, under orders of Gen. Thomas J. "Stonewall" Jackson, to draw straws to figure out which one was to be executed by a firing squad. He and this execution were the subjects of one of the articles from the Heritage & Heraldry column a few years back.

For a great resource with more information on the Pence family, check this website out http://www.pipeline.com/~richardpence/

Early Lineage of the Richards Family of Page County
Article of 6/27/2002

While Germanic influence dominates most of the Page Valley's population, at some point or another, it makes things rather interesting when you can find one of Welsh ancestry. Believed to have been the son of John and Lydia Beaman Richards, Rowland Richards, Sr. was born on May 1, 1660 in Merionshire, North Wales. Apparently, by 1689 he had made his way to Merion Township, Pennsylvania where he married Catherine Jones.

Like Rowland, Catherine was also of Welsh descent. Born June 1668, she was the daughter of Hugh John ap Thomas, who, in turn is believed to have been the son of John Thomas. Rowland, Sr. died November 8, 1720 in Tredyffrin, Montgomery County, Pennsylvania. Catherine followed her husband years later on July 20, 1758 while residing in Chester County, Pennsylvania.

Rowland and Catherine's first child appears to have been Rowland Richards, Jr., born April 22, 1690 in Chester County, Pennsylvania. Rowland, Jr. married Sarah Thomas (also likely of Welsh descent) June 26, 1716.

Finally, after so much begetting reminiscent of the Bible, we get to one of Rowland, Jr. and Sarah Thomas Richards sons, Aquilla Richards. Aquilla leaves a bit more mystery to his appearance on the scene, but was believed to have been born between 1723-1745. At present, I don't have the name of his wife, but by 1790, Aquilla does appear on the census for Robeson Township, Berks County, Pennsylvania. Like generations before him, he too named a son for himself.

Born about 1804, probably in Berks County, Aquilla Richards, Jr. may have been a solitary immigrant to the Shenandoah Valley sometime in the early 1820s (perhaps at first to Frederick County), or he may have moved in the company of other family members. Nevertheless, by 1823, he had moved into the area that later was known as Page County and married Polly Cave. His marriage to Polly was short lived as her death occurred ca. 1825-1826. At least one son, Benjamin, was born from this first marriage in 1825. Aquilla's second marriage was in 1827 to Amelia or "Millie" Cave.

Millie was the illegitimate child of John Keyser (son of Karl Keyser, Sr.) and Polly Cave (not to be confused with Aquilla's first wife as this Polly was born ca. 1770).

After the births of at least five children, the youngest being born in 1845, Aquilla appears to have died before 1850 (as he is also not listed on that year's census for Page County). Children from this marriage included Joseph (1833), Nathaniel (1837), Howard (about 1840), Nancy (1843), and Isabella (1845).

By 1860, only the sons can be easily traced clearly in the census. Benjamin and Howard were working as laborers in Stony Man District #2. Joseph, with the same occupation, was in Luray District #3.

The Stoneberger Family of Page County
Article of 11/08/2001

Believed to be the progenitor of the Page County Stonebergers, Frederick Johann Stoneberger (Steinberger) was probably born ca. 1730 in Germany. After arriving in Philadelphia in 1750, Frederick is believed to have married "Mary."

In all, Frederick and Mary are believed to have had between five and seven children. According to the research of one descendant, two Steinbergers are listed in DAR records (Jost and Lorenz) that were of the right age and location to be children of Frederick. However, they served in Pennsylvania units and there seems to be no census information that helps solidify the possible link. Lorenz is recorded to have lived to the ripe old age of 106!

Of the five known children of Frederick there were Lewis, Christina, John, Dorothy, and Frederick, Jr.

The Frederick Stoneberger family appears to have settled in the Shenandoah Valley near the family of John Christian Nauman. In 1775, sons Frederick, John and Lewis Stoneberger joined and served with Captain Michael Rader's short-lived company. Lewis is the only son known to have later received a pension for his service.

Lewis Stoneberger's widow, the former Mary Ann Finter, applied for a pension in Page County on January 22, 1844 ("under provisions of the Act of Congress passed July 7, 1838, allowing half pay to widows, etc."). According to the pension affidavit, apparently after service in Reader's company, Lewis may have belonged to the same company as Andrew Keyser. In the same statement, his wife also recalled (at ninety years of age) that he had served for three years, marching from Shenandoah County under the command of Captain Peter Printz. After service in the Virginia Militia "at the taking of Cornwallis at Yorktown," Stoneberger's company marched, oddly, to Wheeling, where he was discharged.

A few years after the war, on August 10, 1785 Lewis and Mary were married in Shenandoah County by "one Paul Hinkle, a minister of the gospel." Lewis died in Shenandoah (Page) County on October 20, 1828.

Remarkably, Mary Ann was still alive in 1845 when her pension was reviewed. At that time (and at the remarkable age of 105!) she was residing in Warren County, Missouri. Already receiving a "hefty" $70 per year from the pension, she had reapplied to receive the bounty land "to which she may be entitled under the act approved of March the 3rd, 1855." Children John and Mary Ann Stoneberger affixed their seals beneath that of their mother, perhaps prepared to work this new bounty land.

The DAR Patriot Index lists John Stoneberger (1760-1821) as a private in the Virginia Army and that he married Elizabeth Norman (Nauman).

Over a decade after Yorktown, early records reveal that the St. Luke's Church at Alma, near Stanley (known as the Stoneberger Church) was signed over by Frederick Stoneberger and Matthias Friarmood to John Nowman (Nauman) and Daniel Snyder, trustees of the congregation. According to Harry M. Stricker, this church replaced an earlier one that "stood on Stony Run near where the Honeyville Road crossed the stream, about two miles east of Alma."

Of the Stoneberger daughters, it is known that Dorothy married Jacob Judy and Christina married Johann Christian Nauman.

By 1860, Stonebergers remained heavily concentrated in Alma, but could also be found throughout the county in Grove Hill, East Liberty, Marksville, Valleyburg, and Cedar Point.

A Casualty of War: The Family of George W. Summers, Sr. Article of 11/29/2001

Possibly a descendant of Hans George Sommer, George W. Summers was not as Anglican as the surname may imply at first glimpse. Hans George was born ca. 1713 in the Palatinate and died on April 26, 1787 in Toms Brook, Virginia. Most of Hans' children settled in Frederick, Shenandoah and Augusta County.

The first appearance of George W. Summers in Page County vital records occurs in 1835 with his marriage to Susannah Strickler. Susannah, the daughter of A. and Susan Hollingsworth, was born in Shenandoah County and had, apparently, married a Strickler prior to marrying Summers. By 1845, the Summers family included four daughters and one son.

With the outbreak of the Civil War, George W. Summers, George Sr.'s only son enlisted with Co. D, 7th Virginia Cavalry. By war's end, he would command the company as a captain.

However, the first traumatic episode of war in the Summers family would occur with daughter Mary Summers Strole. By 1862, Hiram and Mary Summers Strole had two wonderful daughters – Amanda Susan (1857) and Mary Lee Virginia (1859). But, in January 1862, not five years old, Amanda died from sickness on the 22nd. Four days later, wife Mary, followed in death. This left only two-year-old Mary Lee with Hiram as the sole parent. It seems unlikely that Hiram would enlist so quickly in the aftermath of such tragedy and, perhaps, he was one to be swept up into the draft that followed early before that spring.

Listed on the rolls of the Page Grays, as a precaution, Hiram made his last will and testament which looked after the well-being of his only daughter in the event of his death – leaving all of his "lands and the benefits thereof." In the event that Mary would die, then all property would be divided among two of his brothers – George and Abraham (later a member of the Purcell Artillery and killed in the trenches of Petersburg in days before the end of the war in 1865) and sister-in-law, Susan.

In the months that followed, Hiram would brave the elements and battles in the Valley, around Richmond and finally, in the fields around Manassas. Though he survived the intensely heated contest at Brawner Farm on August 28, 1862, the following day, during a strong Union attack, Hiram was killed. Captain Michael Shuler wrote that after falling "back a short distance, [they] were not able to get the dead off." Ultimately, Hiram's body was recovered and brought back to Page and buried next to his wife and daughter.

Within days of her third birthday on September 3, Mary was an orphan.

Mary did survive and, with her marriage to Wilson Asbury Koontz in 1878, began another branch of her family that would include six boys and three girls.

The end of the war, as many know, did not bring relief for the Summers family, as, on June 27, 1865, George W., Jr. was executed without trial at Rude's Hill.

Within six years of the end of the tragic war, Susannah Summers died leaving George Sr. with what appears from his writings, to have been a struggle with depression over the loss of his only son. At only 65 years of age, George W. Summers, Sr. died on September 26, 1877.

Miscellaneous

Heritage Tourism in Luray and Page County: How and Why? Article of 5/30/2002

While certainly not the "solves-all" or "one swipe solution" to the unemployment crunch in Page County, heritage tourism is a credible means in bringing about economic development. There are communities across the United States that have taken notice of the potential and made history work for them.

The National Trust for Historic Preservation (NTHP) is a pivotal link in developing such programs. As defined on the NTHP Web site (www.nationaltrust.org): "Heritage tourism is travel that allows visitors to experience the places and activities that authentically represent the stories and people of the past. It is one of the fastest-growing segments of the travel industry, one that can bring many benefits to travelers and to communities."

Additionally, "Heritage tourism can provide a particularly strong boost to a local economy. While the average U.S. traveler spends $425 and 3.3 nights away from home per trip, visitors to historic and cultural attraction sites spend $615 and 4.7 nights. Their spending can help diversify a local community's character. These results are particularly valuable in rural areas, many of which have created successful tourism programs."

As I've said in the past, Luray and Page County, packaged in a particular way, becomes it's own self-contained open-air museum. However, driving by this site or that does not necessarily mean the typical traveler (or even local) knows the history behind the site. Someone might recognize a place and say, "that's a really old house, if those walls could only talk." Ultimately, the house needs help to make that happen and that is found in the form of a strong historic preservation/interpretation advocacy group interested not only in fixing up an old place, but interpreting it for the public and making it a selling point in area tourism. However, sometimes, the cart comes before the horse, in a matter of speaking, in that by interpreting, you form a public concern that leads to preservation.

On the flip side, not everybody wants Joe Q. Public from outside the Old Dominion tramping across their property to see an historic marker and read about the treasures of the house or site upon which it focuses. It doesn't necessarily have to be like that. Rather, it is possible to interpret and appreciate from a distance. That is where the first step in partnerships comes into play. Who is willing to work with your historic preservation advocates to make interpretation and/or preservation a possibility?

What are the parameters of these things and when and how do you prevent them from infringing on landowners' interests? Again, partnerships are key. Make sure that you utilize the resources already in place.

History doesn't have to be merely memorization of important dates and names. With a little work and development, "history" can mean money and jobs.

Site of Summers-Koontz Execution Now Under Protection
Article of 6/3/2004

Two years after a representative of the local Summers-Koontz Camp introduced the Executive Director of the Shenandoah Valley Battlefields Foundation to the landowner of the Shenandoah County property where Page County Confederates Captain George W. Summers and Sgt. Isaac Newton Koontz were executed in a tragic postwar incident, the land has finally come under protection.

In March of this year, the Shenandoah Valley Battlefields Foundation officially closed the purchase on the land that is essentially the north side of what is known as Rude's Hill. Approximately 10-acres, the land encompasses the site where Summers and Koontz were executed on June 27, 1865, however, the battlefield preservation effort was primarily focused on the land for the fact that it is within an area identified a number of years ago as critical or "core" battlefield area related to the Battle of New Market. In the closing hours of the Battle of New Market, in an effort to save the bulk of Union Gen. Franz Sigel's army, Union artillery Captain Henry A. DuPont placed his artillery battery at Rude's Hill and successfully delayed the Confederate pursuit.

The Page County connection with the property is, of course, the story behind the incident wherein Summers and Koontz were executed without trial on June 27, 1865, despite having received assurances that no retribution would come to them for the episode that took place on the Valley Pike on May 22, 1865 between them (Summers, Koontz, Jacob D. Koontz and Andrew Jackson Kite – all former members of Co. D, 7th Virginia Cavalry) and the small band of Federals from the 22nd New York Cavalry. Jacob Koontz and Jackson Kite both evaded execution by having slipped away from their homes, having received enough warning of advancing Federal patrols toward their houses. Capt. Summers and Sgt. Koontz were not told of the orders of execution until they reached Smith Creek in Shenandoah County.

As early as 1893, Thomas Jackson Adams (a former member of Co. K, 23rd Va. Cavalry) had successfully raised enough funds to replace the stump that had previously marked the site of the execution with a small monument. Adams had hoped that the site at Rude's Hill would be "often visited by those who admire courage and fortitude, and the tragic deaths of Capt. Summers and Sergt. Koontz will long live in the memories of our citizens and deserve to be recited in song and story, - to show what atrocities our people suffered in war, and how heroically these men met their untimely fate."

Today, that monument stands over 100 yards back from the Valley Pike (Rt. 11) on the recently purchased property and has not been accessible to travelers for years. However, the SVBF is planning on creating a pull-off and closer access to the monument in the future as well as interpretive signage for the events related to the Battle of New Market. The local Summers-Koontz Camp hopes to work with the SVBF to raise funding to restore the monument. Additionally, while there is a Department of Historic Resources marker standing nearby giving grief interpretation of the tragic event in 1865, the camp would also like to raise sufficient funds to place a Virginia Civil War Trails giving clear details behind the incident. The camp has already been actively involved in placing several Virginia Civil War Trails markers in Page County and has plans for more in the future – continuously taking an active role in heritage tourism in the area.

The Fate of Historic Overall Pass and Milford (September 1864) Article of 5/16/2002

On Wednesday night, May 22, there will be a hearing at Luray High School about the final decision of the fate of Rt. 340 between Overall and Rileyville. At 8 p.m., folks will have their last opportunity to make comments or ask questions.

Overall/Milford was the site of Page County's largest military action during the Civil War. Certainly, there are some that say, "aren't there enough battlefields preserved already?"

First, Page doesn't have a preserved battle site, rather, it has interpreted segments of Civil War history through the Virginia Civil War Trails markers in the county. But it's also not just about saving a battlefield. Often, like most things, it's what you make of things afterwards that makes a difference.

First, protection of important sites, like Milford, should be considered. In turn, this should be followed by a sound plan for preservation and interpretation. Not just for the many tourists that come to the Shenandoah Valley every year, but also for the local population, and especially our children and generations to come. But, as I said, it doesn't have to stop there. Without destroying the landscape or the personal character that so many want to come and see, interpret the historic site with economic development in mind. With the worries of unemployment on the minds of many, turn historic assets into something else. Not to the point of Gettysburg-level commercialization, but make it a part of a destination that is both tasteful and encourages the average hotel or B&B visitor to spend at least one more night, dine at local restaurants another day and descend upon the many treasures offered by a variety of local retailers.

Historic Milford was a quiet little place before the Civil War. As the war erupted, the area around Milford was found to be a perfect "choke-point," militarily speaking. The ground around Milford offered excellent defensible heights and fantastic natural flanks with the South Fork of the Shenandoah on one side and the Blue Ridge Mountains on the other. Though it did not appear then as now (especially the modern abundance of foliage), the terrain was not hospitable to the typical Civil War military action that so many read about.

"Overall Pass," as some referred to it, saw a variety of historical characters visit and experience the immediate area over time. During the Civil War notables such as Confederate General Stonewall Jackson, Union General James Shields, and mapmaker Jedediah Hotchkiss glanced upon the landscape around Milford. In 1864, Milford/Overall bore witness to an action at which even George Custer was present. The September fight is significant in that it likely saved General Jubal Early's Confederate army from annihilation following the battle of Fisher's Hill.

If you're concerned about saving a significant Page County historical and scenic treasure, May 22 might be your last opportunity to speak out.

Index

About the Author

A native of Page County, Virginia, Robert H. Moore, II completed most of his undergraduate work at East Carolina University and received his Bachelor of Science degree in Liberal Studies from Excelsior College in 1995. He completed graduate coursework in History at Old Dominion University. Robert has written seven books for the Virginia Regimental History Series and, most recently, has published *Avenue of Armies: Civil War Sites and Stories of Page County,* Virginia and *Gibraltar of the Shenandoah: Civil War Sites and Stories of Staunton, Waynesboro and Augusta County, Virginia.* He has also written for magazines such as *Civil War Times Illustrated, Blue and Gray Magazine* and *America's Civil War.* For the past seven years, Robert has also maintained the "Heritage and Heraldry" newspaper column for the *Page News & Courier.* He is presently the Commander of the Summers-Koontz Camp #490, Sons of Confederate Veterans in Luray. He currently resides with his family in Augusta County.

www.ingramcontent.com/pod-product-compliance
Lightning Source LLC
LaVergne TN
LVHW050623100826
845148LV00011B/1709

9780788435942